University College Worcester
Library
Henwick Grove, WORCESTER, WR2 6AJ

D0997909

Key Geography Connections

David Waugh
Former Head of Geography
Trinity School
Carlisle

Tony Bushell
Head of Geography
West Gate Community College
Newcastle upon Tyne

Stanley Thornes (Publishers) Ltd

A1012835

Text © David Waugh, Tony Bushell, 1992, 1997
Original line illustrations © Stanley Thornes (Publishers) Ltd 1992, 1997

Second edition designed and typeset by Hilary Norman
Illustrations by Kathy Baxendale, Nick Hawken, Malcolm Porter, Tim Smith, John Yorke
Cartoons by Mike Gordon
Edited by Katherine James
Photo research by Julia Hanson

All rights reserved. No part of this publication may be reproduced or transmitted in any form or by any means, electronic or mechanical, including photocopy, recording or any information storage and retrieval system, without permission in writing from the publisher or under licence from the Copyright Licensing Agency Limited. Further details of such licences (for reprographic reproduction) may be obtained from the Copyright Licensing Agency Limited, of 90 Tottenham Court Road, London W1P 9HE.

First published in 1992 and reprinted eight times.
Second edition published in 1997 by:
Stanley Thornes (Publishers) Ltd
Ellenborough House
Wellington Street
CHELTENHAM GL50 1YD
England

99 00 / 10 9 8 7 6

A catalogue record for this book is available from the British Library

First edition ISBN 0-7487-1102-3
Second edition ISBN 0-7487-2880-5

Printed in China

The previous page shows Adelie penguins near Faraday Base, Antarctica

A 1012835

Resource Area
910 KEY

Acknowledgements

The authors and publishers are grateful to the following for permission to reproduce photographs and other material in this book.

Aerofilms, p. 13; Art Directors, pp. 27, 62 bottom left; John Beatty, p. 20 bottom right; Bradford Libraries and Information Services, p. 40; British Antarctic Survey, pp. 54 bottom, 55 both; British Coal, p. 20 bottom left; British Petroleum Company plc, p. 58 top; British Steel, p. 35 top; Bruce Coleman Ltd, pp. 52 top left, bottom centre, bottom right, 53 top right, 54 top, 58 bottom, 84 top; Colorific!, p. 62 top right; Countryside Commission, p.14; Eye Ubiquitous, pp. 32 (J. Edkins), 34 bottom right (David Langfield), 50 left (A. Oldfield), centre (C. Bland), right (D. Gill); FLPA, pp. 6 top left, 26 top left, 66 bottom left, 72 bottom block – top left and bottom right; Leslie Garland, p. 17; Robert Harding Picture Library, pp. 6 bottom right (Gavin Heller), 11, 62 bottom right, 72 top, 88 left (Nigel Francis), 89 top (Gavin Heller); Holt Studios, p. 28 bottom; The Hutchison Library, pp. 26 right, 53 bottom right; IBM UK Ltd, p. 42; ICCE Picture Library, pp. 5 top right, 20 top left, 31 top, 52 bottom left, top centre and top right; National Power, p. 60; National Rivers Authority, p. 16; Oxford Scientific Films, p. 31 bottom; Panos Pictures, pp. 26 bottom left, 66 bottom right; David Paterson, pp. 4 top left, 6 top right, 66 top left; Rochdale Libraries, p. 34 top left; Science Photo Library, pp. 28 top, 34 top right, 46 all, 62 top left, 66 top centre, 68; Peter Smith Photography, Malton, pp. 15, 97 left; Spectrum Colour Library, pp. 24 left, 92 top; Tony Stone Images, pp. 6 bottom left, 72 bottom block – centre left and centre right; Sygma, p. 59 both; Toyota GB Ltd. p. 101; Tropix, p. 93 bottom; Charles Tustian, p. 20 centre right; Vauxhall Motors, p. 34 bottom left; Tony Waltham, Geophotos, pp. 4 top centre, top right, bottom right, 21 centre, 22 top, 24 right, 97 right; Simon Warner, pp. 21 top and bottom, 66 top right; Judith Waugh, p. 85 (right); Mike Williams, p. 29.

All other photographs were supplied by the authors

Every effort has been made to contact copyright holders and we apologise if any have been overlooked.

Contents

What is weathering?

There is a great variety of different scenery in the world. Some places are mountainous, some are flat, some can be described as spectacular and others simply as interesting. Geographers call the scenery of a place the **landscape**. Some examples of the world's landscapes are shown in photos **A**, **B** and **C**.

The surface of the earth and the landscapes we see around us not only differ from place to place, but they are changing all the time.

Rain, sun, wind and frost constantly break down the rocks. Great mountain ranges get worn down, valleys are made wider and deeper, and coastlines are changed. The breaking up of the earth's surface in this way is due to **weathering** and **erosion**. Weathering takes place when the rocks are attacked by the weather. Erosion is the wearing away of the land. These two pages show some examples of weathering. Erosion is explained more fully on pages 6 and 7.

A Mount Everest

B Monument Valley, USA

C Guilin, China

Freeze–thaw weathering

This can also be called frost shattering. Water may get into a crack in a rock and freeze. As the water turns to ice it expands and causes the crack to open a little. When it thaws the ice melts and changes back to water. Repeated freezing and thawing weakens the rock and splits it into jagged pieces. This type of weathering is common in mountainous areas where temperatures are often around freezing point.

Water fills a crack in a rock

The water freezes and the crack is made wider

The rock breaks into several pieces

Onion-skin weathering

This happens when a rock is repeatedly heated and cooled. As it is heated, the outer layer of the rock expands slightly and as it cools the rock contracts. Continual expansion and contraction causes small pieces of the rock surface to peel off like the skin of an onion. This type of weathering is common in desert areas where it is very hot during the day but cool at night.

Biological weathering

This is due to the action of plants and animals. Seeds may fall into cracks in the rocks where shelter and moisture help them grow into small plants or trees. As the roots develop they gradually force the cracks to widen and the rock to fall apart. Eventually whole rocks can be broken into small pieces. Burrowing animals such as rabbits, moles and even earthworms can also help break down rock.

Chemical weathering

This is caused by the action of water. Ordinary rainwater contains small amounts of acid. When it comes into contact with rock the acid attacks it and causes the rock to rot and crumble away. The results of this can be seen on buildings and in churchyards where the stone has been worn away or pitted. Water and heat make chemical weathering happen faster, so it is greatest in places that are warm and wet.

Activities

1 Make a larger copy of diagram **D**.
   a) Write in the meaning of weathering.
   b) Add labels to the weathering features.

Weathering is _____

2 Copy and complete these sentences.
   a) Freeze–thaw weathering is . . .
   b) Onion-skin weathering is . . .
   c) Chemical weathering is . . .

3 With the help of a labelled diagram show how freeze–thaw weathering can break up rocks.

4 **a)** Make a larger copy of diagram **E**.
   b) Show how root action can break up rocks, by adding the following labels to the correct boxes. Give your diagram a title.

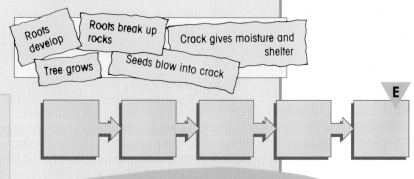

Roots develop

Roots break up rocks

Crack gives moisture and shelter

Tree grows

Seeds blow into crack

E

EXTRA

Draw these simple sketches of photos **A**, **B** and **C**. Give each sketch a title and underneath say what type of weathering is likely to be most important there. Give reasons for your answers.

Summary

Weathering is the breakdown of rocks by water, frost and temperature change. Rocks can also be broken down by the effects of plants and animals.

What is erosion . . .

Weathering and erosion work together. Weathering breaks up and weakens the surface of rocks while erosion wears away and removes the loosened material. The action of rivers, the sea, ice and wind are the chief types of erosion. Human erosion is also important. Bulldozers and lorries can dig out and move large amounts of soil and loose rock, so changing the landscape. People also remove trees and vegetation which can allow water, wind and ice to erode land more easily.

The work of rivers, the sea, ice and wind are explained in **A** below.

A

Rivers

Every day rivers wear away tiny bits of rock from their bed, and eat into the banks on either side of the channel. This material is carried downstream and deposited when the water slows down. In times of flood large boulders may be loosened and rolled down the river bed.

Ice

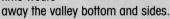

A **glacier** is a tongue of ice moving down a valley. Stones and boulders that fall on to it freeze into the ice and act like sandpaper on the rocks beneath. As the glacier moves, it carries the material downwards and at the same time wears away the valley bottom and sides.

Sea

Coastlines are under constant attack by **waves**. During storms each wave hits the rock with a weight of several tonnes. When this is repeated many times, the rock is weakened and pieces break off. **Currents** carry loose material away and deposit it elsewhere.

Wind

Explorers who cross deserts in cars often find their paintwork worn away and their windscreens scratched. This is because the wind picks up tiny particles of sand and blasts them against anything that is in the way. Rocks in desert areas are often eroded into strange shapes by this sand-blasting effect.

... and how can it help shape the land?

Look at cartoon **B** on the right. It shows some gardeners who are trying to alter a garden by digging out soil (erosion), moving it in a wheelbarrow (transportation), and dumping it somewhere else (deposition). The more energy they have, the more soil they can dig or transport. When they are tired the digging slows down and they lack the strength to push the barrow, resulting in it toppling over and dumping its load.

On a larger scale, mountains, valleys, plains and coasts are shaped and changed by water, ice and wind. **Erosion** wears away the land, **transportation** moves the material from one place to another, and **deposition** builds up new landforms.

B

EROSION... ➡ TRANSPORTATION ➡ DEPOSITION

Activities

1 **a)** List the following in order of how hard they are. Give the hardest first and the softest last.

| steel | chalk | soap | wood |

| rubber | diamond | plastic |

b) Put a line under the two you think would be the most difficult to wear down.
c) Choose any three from your list and say how they might be worn down.

2 Of the five statements below, three are correct. Write out the correct ones.
   ● Weathering is the breakdown of rock by nature.
   ● Erosion is the wearing away of rock.
   ● Weathering and erosion are the same.
   ● Weathering moves material from one place to another.
   ● Erosion includes the removal of loose material.

3 **a)** Make a large copy of table **C**.
   b) Add labels to each drawing.
   c) Write a short description for each type of erosion.

E X T R A

Cartoon **B** shows erosion, transportation and deposition in a garden. How else could this be shown? What about a bulldozer, washing dishes or sandpapering wood? For one of these ideas, or for one of your own, draw a simple labelled cartoon to show how it works.

C Types of erosion

Type	Description

Summary Erosion is the wearing away of rock and its removal by streams, ice, waves and wind. Erosion, transportation and deposition help shape the land.

How do rivers shape the land?

Rivers work hard. They hardly stop and they continually erode and move material downstream. They are a major force in shaping and altering the land. Running water by itself actually has little power to wear away rocks. What happens is that the water pushes boulders, stones and rock particles along the river's course. As it does so, the loose material scrapes the river bed and banks and loosens other material. Much of what is worn away is then transported by the river and put down somewhere else. In this way rivers can wear out and deepen valleys. They can also change their shape by depositing material.

The landforms to be seen along a river change as it flows from source to mouth. These two pages explain the features of a river in its upper course which is usually in the hills or mountains. Diagram **A** and photo **B** show how a river cuts out a steep-sided valley that is V-shaped.

A

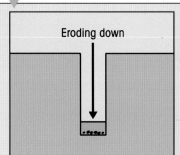 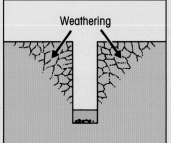 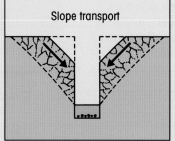 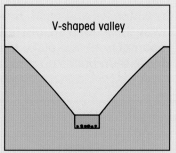

| Eroding down | Weathering | Slope transport | V-shaped valley |

1 The river erodes downwards as boulders, stones and rock particles are bounced and scraped along the channel bed.

2 As the river cuts down, the steep sides are attacked by weathering. This breaks up and loosens the soil and rock.

3 The loosened material slowly creeps down the slope because of gravity or is washed into the river by rainwater. The river carries it away.

4 The end result is a steep-sided valley that has the shape of a letter 'V'.

B

The making of a V-shaped valley

Slopes attacked by weathering

River erodes downwards

Gravity and rainwater move material downwards (slope transport)

River source

V-shaped valley

Rocks and pebbles moved along the bed

Weathered and eroded material transported by river

Table **C** below and sketch **D** give some features of a river and its valley.

C

Source	Where a river starts
Spurs	Ridges of land around which a river winds
Valley sides	The slopes on either side of a river
V-shaped valley	The shape of a valley in its upper course
Channel	The course of a river
River banks	The sides of a river channel
River bed	The bottom of a river channel
Load	Material that is carried or moved by the river

D

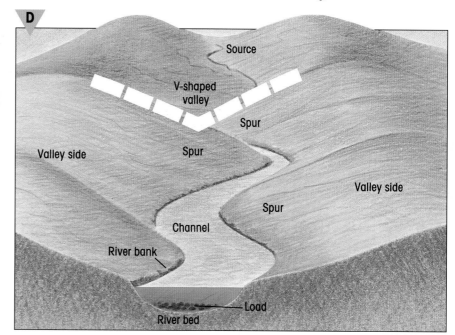

Activities

1 Describe how rivers erode their channels. Include these words in your description:

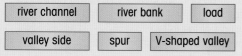

pushes scrapes loosens moves drops

2 **a)** Make a large copy of diagram **E**.
 b) Show how a valley gets to be V-shaped by describing what happens at ①, ②, ③ and ④.
 c) Give your diagram a suitable title.

E

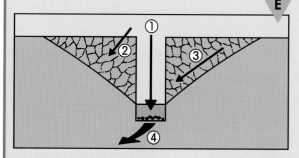

3 **a)** Sketch **F** is a simplified drawing of the river valley shown in photo **B**. Make a copy of the sketch.
 b) Add the terms below to your sketch in the correct places. The information at the top of this page will help you.

river channel river bank load

valley side spur V-shaped valley

F

Summary Rivers erode, transport and deposit material. This helps shape the land. V-shaped valleys are a common feature of a river in its upper course.

What causes waterfalls?

A

979 m
Angel Falls

244 m
Canary Wharf Tower

Niagara Falls

50 m
High Force
20 m

Waterfalls are an attractive and often spectacular feature of a river. The highest waterfall in the world is the Angel Falls in South America. Its total height is 979 metres. That is about four times the height of Britain's tallest building, the Canary Wharf Tower in London's Docklands. Waterfalls in Britain are much smaller than this (diagram **A**). One of the finest is High Force in the north of England. It has a height of just 20 metres. It is most impressive in times of flood.

Probably the best known waterfall in the world is Niagara Falls. It lies on the Niagara River which forms part of the border between Canada and the United States. In this area, a band of hard limestone rock lies on top of softer shales and sandstone. The river flows over the top of the hard rock then plunges down a 50 metre cliff. At the bottom of the cliff the water has worn away the softer rocks to form a pool over 50 metres deep. This is called a **plunge pool**. Down from the falls is the Niagara Gorge. A **gorge** is a valley with almost vertical sides that has been carved out by the river and the waterfall. Photo **D** shows the gorge and waterfall at Niagara.

Sketch **B** shows the Niagara Falls area. The falls here are eating into the cliffs behind the waterfall at nearly one metre a year. The gorge that has been left behind is now 11 kilometres long.

Many waterfalls are formed in the same way as Niagara. They occur when rivers flow over different types of rock. The soft rock wears away faster than the hard rock. In time a step develops over which the river plunges as a waterfall. Water also cuts away rock behind the waterfall. This causes the falls to move back and leave a gorge as it goes. Diagram **C** shows how a waterfall may be worn away by a river.

B

Lake Erie

CANADA

Niagara River

Goat Island

Horseshoe Falls

UNITED STATES OF AMERICA

American Falls

Original position of falls

Niagara Gorge

11 km

CANADA

N

Hard rock
Soft rock

C

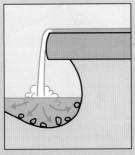

River

Hard rock

Soft rock

Plunge pool

1 Falling water and rock particles or boulders loosen and wear away the softer rock.

2 The hard rock above is undercut as erosion of the soft rock continues.

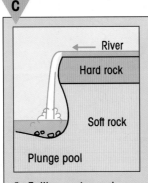

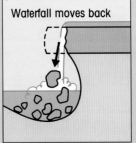

Waterfall moves back

3 The hard rock collapses into the plunge pool to be broken up and washed away by the river. The position of the falls moves back.

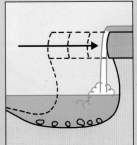

4 Erosion continues and the waterfall slowly eats its way upstream, leaving a gorge behind.

Activities

1 Map **E** shows the Niagara Falls area.
  a) Make an accurate copy of the map.
  b) Colour the water blue and the land area green.
  c) Label the following:

| USA | Canada | American Falls | Niagara River |

| Horseshoe Falls | Niagara Gorge | Goat Island |

  d) Draw on and label the original position of the falls.
  e) The falls have taken 30,000 years to wear back 11 km. Draw on and label where the falls might be 10,000 years from now.

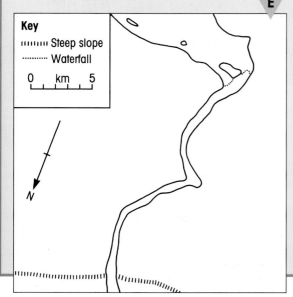

Key
~~~~~~~ Steep slope
------- Waterfall

0   km   5

N

2 a) Make a larger copy of diagram **F**.
  b) Put these labels in the correct places.

| Hard rock | Soft rock | Plunge pool |

| Hard rock breaks off | Eroded material |

| Undercutting | Waterfall moves back |

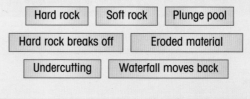

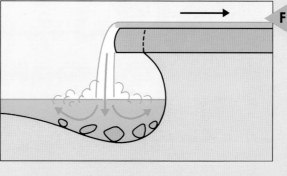

3 Sort the phrases in **G** into the correct order and link them with arrows to show how a waterfall may be worn away by a river.

Hard rock collapses
Plunge pool deepened
Soft rock worn away
Waterfall moves back
Hard rock undercut

Summary

Many waterfalls are a result of water wearing away soft rock more quickly than hard rock. As a waterfall erodes back, a gorge may be produced.

What happens on a river bend?

Have you noticed that rivers rarely flow in a straight line? Usually they twist and turn as they make their way down to the sea. The only time they are straight seems to be when people interfere with them by building banks or diverting their course.

Bends develop on a river mainly because of the water's eroding power. Think about when you are a passenger in a car and it goes around a corner. You are thrown towards the outside of the curve, often with quite a lot of force. The same happens when a river goes around a bend. The force of the water is greatest towards the outside of the bend. When it hits the bank it causes erosion. This erosion deepens the channel at that point and wears away the bank to make a small **river cliff**. On the inside of the bend, water movement is slower. Material builds up here due to deposition. This makes the bank gently sloping and the river channel shallow.

Diagram **A** shows what happens on a river bend. At the bottom of the diagram is a **cross-section**. This shows what the river would look like if a slice was cut across it from one side to the other.

A

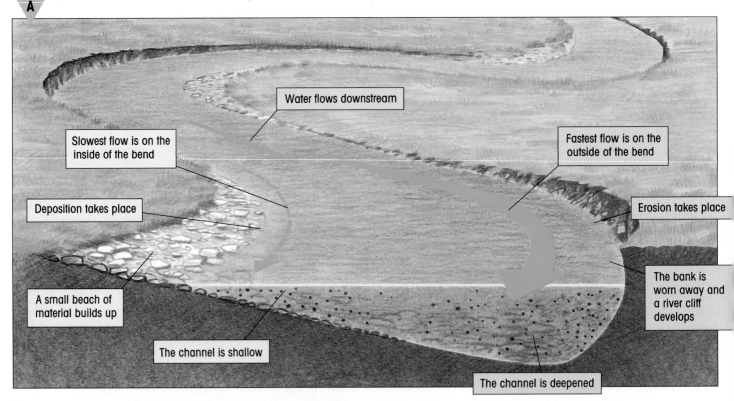

Water flows downstream

Slowest flow is on the inside of the bend

Fastest flow is on the outside of the bend

Deposition takes place

Erosion takes place

A small beach of material builds up

The bank is worn away and a river cliff develops

The channel is shallow

The channel is deepened

B

Deposition on the inside of a river bend

C

Erosion on the outside of a river bend

Look at sketch **D** and photo **E**. The river has many bends. These are called **meanders** and are a common feature of most rivers. On either side of the river channel there is an area of flat land called the **flood plain**. This area gets covered in water when the river overflows its banks. Flood plains are made up of **alluvium**, a fine muddy material that is left behind after floods. Alluvium is sometimes called **silt**.

Flood plains are useful to people because they are areas of flat land and have rich fertile soil. This makes them good for building on and for farming.

E

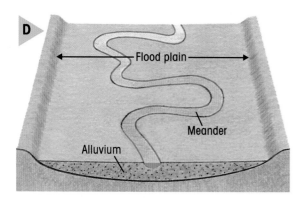

D

Flood plain

Meander

Alluvium

Activities

1 Look at diagram **F**, which is a simple cross-section of a river bend.
   a) Draw the cross-section.
   b) Write the labels from **G** in the correct places.
   c) Give your drawing a title.
   d) Describe why one side of the river bend is different from the other.

2 a) Make simple sketches of photos **B** and **C**.
   b) For each sketch describe the river feature that it shows.
   c) Explain how each feature was made.

3 Give the meaning of the terms shown in sketch **D**.

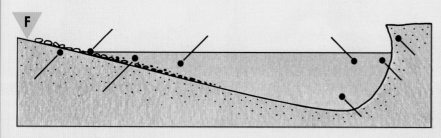

F

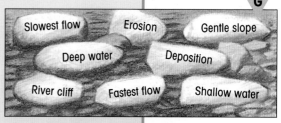

G

Slowest flow   Erosion   Gentle slope

Deep water   Deposition

River cliff   Fastest flow   Shallow water

E X T R A S

1 Write down two reasons why the flood plain of a valley is good for farming.

2 Give one problem of farming the flood plain. Suggest what could be done to reduce the problem.

Summary

A river's course is seldom straight. It usually has many bends which cause it to meander down its valley. The outside of a river bend is worn away by erosion while the inside is built up by deposition.

How does the sea shape the coast?

The sea is never still. On quiet days the movement is slow and gentle, and the sea is flat and almost calm. On stormy days large waves crash against the shore. These large waves have such force that they can drive a ship against the rocks or smash up sea defences and piers. The sea can also wear away the coast and move bits of rock and sand from one place to another. This ability to erode, transport and deposit material produces many interesting coastal landforms.

Erosion landforms are made by the wearing away of the coast (photo **A**). In stormy conditions the sea picks up loose rocks and throws them at the shore. This bombardment undercuts cliffs, opens up cracks and breaks up loose rocks into smaller and smaller pieces. Areas which have soft rocks are worn away more easily than those with hard rocks. The soft rock areas become **bays** and the hard rock areas become **headlands**. A bay is an opening in the coastline. A headland is a stretch of land jutting out into the sea.

A Old Harry Rocks, the Foreland, Dorset

Sketch **B** shows how a headland is eroded by the sea and how other landforms develop.

B

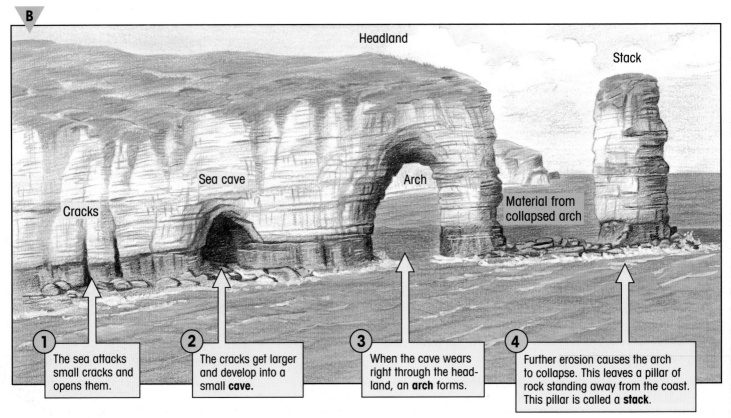

Headland

Stack

Sea cave

Arch

Material from collapsed arch

Cracks

① The sea attacks small cracks and opens them.

② The cracks get larger and develop into a small **cave.**

③ When the cave wears right through the headland, an **arch** forms.

④ Further erosion causes the arch to collapse. This leaves a pillar of rock standing away from the coast. This pillar is called a **stack.**

14

Beaches are one of the most common features of our shoreline. They are formed when material worn away from one part of the coast is carried along and dropped somewhere else. A beach is an example of a **deposition landform**. A **spit** is a special type of beach extending out into the sea. It is a long finger of sand and shingle that often grows out across a bay or the mouth of a river.

Photo **C** and map **D** show Spurn Head spit. It is 6 kilometres long and forms a sweeping curve that stretches halfway across the mouth of the River Humber. It is continually changing its shape as new material is deposited and old material is worn away or moved elsewhere.

C

The making of Spurn Head spit

1 Erosion of coastline north of Spurn Head

2 Eroded material transported down the coast by sea currents

3 Material dropped where coastline changes direction

4 Spit grows out from coast as more material builds up

5 End of spit curved by action of the waves.

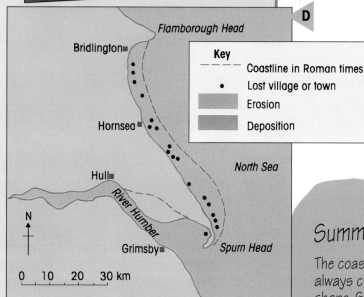

River Humber

North Sea

Activities

1 **a)** Make a sketch of photo **A**.
   b) Mark and label on your sketch the following terms:

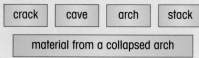

   | crack | cave | arch | stack |

   | material from a collapsed arch |

   c) Give your sketch a title.

2 **a)** Copy map **D** showing the Spurn Head area.
   b) Shade **orange** the area of coastal erosion from Flamborough Head to the northern end of Spurn Head.
   c) Shade **purple** the areas of deposition on Spurn Head and in the mouth of the Humber.
   d) Draw an arrow to show the movement of eroded material along the coast.

3 **a)** Explain why some of the villages on map **D** have been 'lost'.
   b) How has the shape of the mouth of the Humber changed since Roman times?

D

Flamborough Head

Bridlington

Key
--- Coastline in Roman times
• Lost village or town
Erosion
Deposition

Hornsea

North Sea

Hull

River Humber

N

Grimsby

Spurn Head

0   10   20   30 km

4 Explain how the spit at Spurn Head has been made. Include these terms in your writing.
   erosion • Flamborough Head • transportation • currents • deposition • Spurn Head • grows • 6 km

Summary

The coastline is always changing its shape. Some parts are being worn away by erosion while other parts are being built up by deposition.

How are rivers polluted?

Water is one of the basic needs of human life and for this reason rivers have long been good places to locate towns and cities. Rivers can provide water for domestic use and supply the needs of industry and agriculture. They may also be used for communications, for the generation of power and, more recently, for recreational purposes. Sadly, they are also used for the disposal of unwanted waste. Waste that is put into rivers from farmland or from cities is continually carried away but there is a limit to how much a river can get rid of. When the limit is reached there is a serious **pollution** problem.

The River Tyne is an example of a polluted river. Most of its pollution comes from the large industrial towns of Newcastle upon Tyne and Gateshead. As map **A** shows, raw sewage from nearly a million people as well as waste from scores of factories was dumped directly into the river. The result was unpleasant sights and smells, danger to public health from poisons in the water, and a biologically dead river that was unable to support fish or any other sort of life.

A

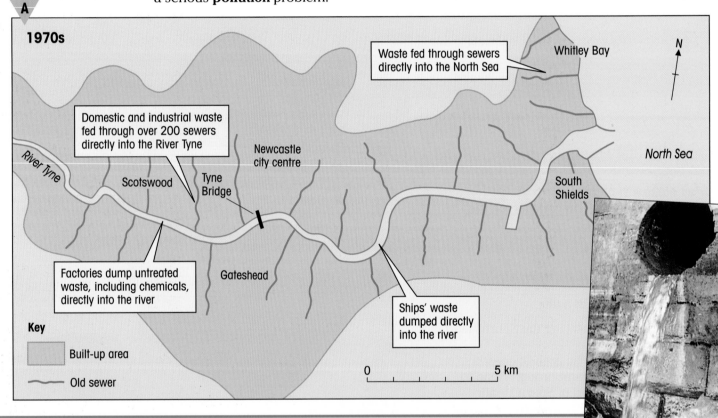

1970s

Waste fed through sewers directly into the North Sea

Whitley Bay

N

Domestic and industrial waste fed through over 200 sewers directly into the River Tyne

Newcastle city centre

North Sea

River Tyne

Scotswood

Tyne Bridge

South Shields

Factories dump untreated waste, including chemicals, directly into the river

Gateshead

Ships' waste dumped directly into the river

Key

Built-up area

Old sewer

0   5 km

Activities

WARNING

1. Give **six** reasons why many towns and cities are located beside rivers.

2. Draw a warning poster to be placed along the banks of the Tyne showing the dangers of pollution in the 1970s. Your poster should show the facts, be colourful and attract attention.

3. Imagine that you work for a pollution research unit. Write a short report to the National Rivers Authority giving the main causes of pollution on the River Tyne. Use the headings *Domestic*, *Industrial* and *Shipping* for your report. Make your report about a page long.

4. Describe the River Tyne clean-up scheme by writing out the following in the correct order. Start with 'Domestic waste . . .' and end with '. . . and fish return.'

And how can they be cleaned up?

On a hot day in the summer of 1969 a Council meeting held near the River Tyne had to be stopped because the smell from the river was so bad. The river today is very different. It is clean, attractive and an ideal place for water sports like sailing, rowing, powerboat racing and windsurfing. It is also reckoned to be one of the best salmon fishing rivers in England.

This dramatic improvement has been brought about in two main ways:

● first, by stopping industry from dumping waste directly into the river
● second, by setting up a huge £150 million clean-up scheme involving the construction of 73 km of new sewers. The scheme is explained in map **C**.

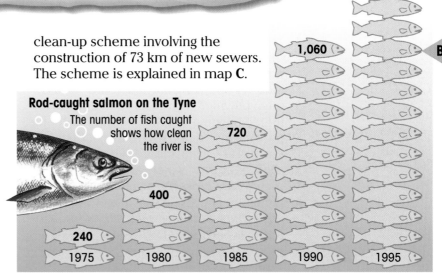

Rod-caught salmon on the Tyne
The number of fish caught shows how clean the river is

1975	1980	1985	1990	1995
240	400	720	1,060	1,380

B

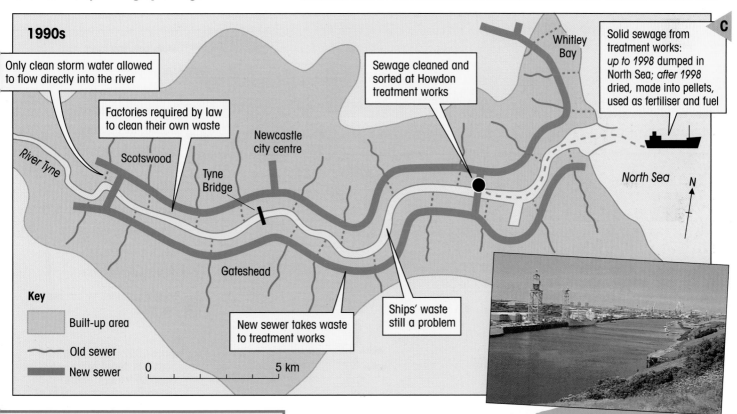

1990s **C**

Only clean storm water allowed to flow directly into the river

Factories required by law to clean their own waste

Sewage cleaned and sorted at Howdon treatment works

Solid sewage from treatment works: *up to 1998* dumped in North Sea; *after 1998* dried, made into pellets, used as fertiliser and fuel

Whitley Bay

Newcastle city centre

River Tyne

Scotswood

Tyne Bridge

North Sea

N

Gateshead

New sewer takes waste to treatment works

Ships' waste still a problem

Key

Built-up area

~~~ Old sewer

▬ New sewer

0   5 km

Add a title to your completed description.
● Domestic waste from houses
● Clean water is returned to the river
● flows down the new sewer to
● so the river quality improves
● goes into the sewers then
● the treatment works.
● and fish return.

EXTRA

For a polluted stream, river or lake that you know:
■ Say what the pollution problem is.
■ Describe the causes of pollution.
■ Suggest how the pollution problem may be reduced.

Summary

Rivers can be very useful to people but their misuse may lead to pollution. Clean-up schemes and regulations to control waste disposal are needed to reduce river pollution.

17

The North Sea – Europe's dustbin

The North Sea is very important. Over 50 million people live close to its shores and no other sea in the world has so much industry operating around it. The sea is a great provider. It gives us sand and gravel for the building industry, cooling water for power stations and fish for food. Coal, oil and gas are extracted from below its shallow, stormy waters and busy shipping routes criss-cross the sea from one side to the other. The sea is also important for recreation – a place to sail on, swim in, or simply a place to relax beside.

Unfortunately the North Sea is also filthy. In fact, it is one of the dirtiest and most polluted of all the seas in the world. It has been called 'Europe's dustbin' because everyone dumps their unwanted rubbish into it. It is estimated that over one billion tonnes of pollution enter the sea every year. Poisonous chemicals, domestic sewage, oil, litter and even radioactive waste all get dumped into the sea.

Some of the causes and effects of this pollution are shown in map **A** below.

A

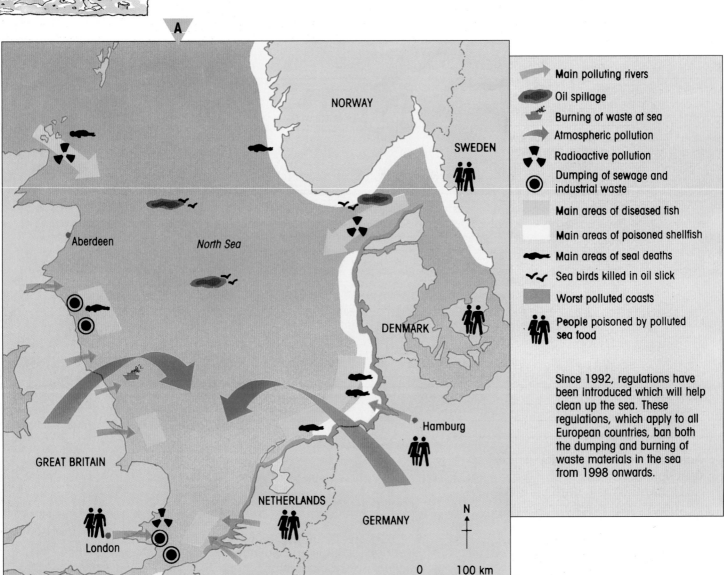

Legend:
- Main polluting rivers
- Oil spillage
- Burning of waste at sea
- Atmospheric pollution
- Radioactive pollution
- Dumping of sewage and industrial waste
- Main areas of diseased fish
- Main areas of poisoned shellfish
- Main areas of seal deaths
- Sea birds killed in oil slick
- Worst polluted coasts
- People poisoned by polluted sea food

Since 1992, regulations have been introduced which will help clean up the sea. These regulations, which apply to all European countries, ban both the dumping and burning of waste materials in the sea from 1998 onwards.

Cleaning up the North Sea is very difficult. We do not know exactly what is dumped in the sea or what actual damage it does. Nor do we know how to clean up the sea or stop people dirtying it. Eight different countries border the North Sea and each blames the other for being the worst polluter. How can laws be made which will be accepted by all? Cleaning up a mess is never easy but unless something is done soon, the damage to the sea will be so great that it may never recover.

Look at diagram **B**. It shows some of the solutions and problems of cleaning up the North Sea.

Activities

1 **a)** Name the countries that have coastlines on the North Sea.
   b) Which countries suffer the worst coastal pollution?

2 Draw table **C** below, and complete it by writing in six causes and six effects of North Sea pollution.
   Note – there is no need to link each cause with an effect.

C

North Sea pollution	
Causes	Effects

3 A ship has to take some cargo from Aberdeen down the east coast of Britain to London. From there it has to sail across to Hamburg in Germany. Follow the ship's route on map **A** and list the types of pollution it will pass through.

4 Give six reasons why it is difficult to clean up the North Sea.

EXTRAS

1 Imagine that you are taking part in a march against North Sea pollution.
   ■ Design a banner to take with you.
   ■ On the banner give suggestions as to how the sea might be cleaned up.
   ■ Add drawings and colour to make your banner interesting and attractive.

2 Draw the flags from diagram **B** and match each one to a North Sea country.

Summary

The North Sea is badly polluted. Pollution comes from rivers, coastal discharges, the air and dumping at sea. Solving the problem of pollution is difficult and needs the joint efforts of many countries.

What are primary industries?

Economic activities are ways by which people can earn their living. One of these groups of economic activity is called **primary industry**. Primary industry is when people collect and use **natural resources**. These natural resources are sometimes called **raw materials**. We get raw materials from the natural (physical) environment of the earth and the sea. There are four main types of primary industry. They are shown on photos **A**, **B**, **C** and **D**.

A

I am a forestry worker. I look after trees until they are ready to chop down.

I am a farmer. I look after animals and grow crops.

B

C

I am a fisherman. I earn my living working at sea.

I am a miner and he is a quarry worker. We get raw materials from either the earth's surface or from underground.

D

How can collecting natural resources harm the environment?

The **mining** of coal, the **quarrying** of slate and the collection of gravel all provide jobs for local people and earn money for the country. However, the collection of natural resources from the ground has bad points as well as good points. Photo **E** is a quarry in a National Park. It has been labelled to show some of the bad effects it has upon the landscape, the local people and the wildlife.

Photo **F** shows an old gravel quarry. Gravel is used in the building industry. Photo **G** shows a coal **spoil tip**. Sometimes when a useful natural resource is collected so too is material for which we have no use. This waste material has to be dumped and forms spoil tips.

Loose rock can be dangerous

Loss of farmland

Noise and vibrations from blasting affects wildlife and buildings

Dust from blasting causes air pollution

Loss of grass and trees where wildlife used to live

Heavy lorries cause noise and air pollution and can make narrow country roads dangerous

Ugly buildings spoil the scenery

Activities

1 What do we mean by a 'primary industry'?

2 Which of the following jobs are primary activities?

| sheep farmer | doctor | coal miner |
| shopkeeper | lorry driver | forestry worker |

3 Copy table **H** below. Complete it with the help of photo **E**. Your completed table should show how quarrying can harm the landscape and affect people and wildlife.

Harmful effects of quarrying on:		
Landscape	People	Wildlife

For either photo **F**, photo **G** or an example in your home area, give **three** ways by which mining or collecting gravel can affect the landscape, people and wildlife.

Summary

Primary industries are when people collect and use natural resources. The collecting of natural resources can harm the landscape and affect people and wildlife.

EXTRA

How can damaged environments be improved?

Old quarries, spoil tips and gravel tips are not very attractive. They can also be very dangerous. As our interest in the environment grows, more attempts are being made to improve these unsightly areas and if possible make them useful again.

A

Photo **A** shows an old gravel pit that has been improved. The ground has been made safe, the water cleaned and the lake converted into a water sports area. Other gravel pits in Britain have been turned into nature reserves.

Spoil tips result from mining and quarrying. In 1966 one tip at Aberfan in South Wales became so wet after heavy rain that it flowed downhill. It covered a primary school and some cottages. Of the 147 people killed, 116 were children. Since then the steep sides of many spoil tips have been made more gentle and have been planted with trees and grass (diagram **B**).

Quarries are often found in National Parks and other attractive areas of countryside. Quarries have now to be landscaped and screened while they are being used (sketch **C**). When quarrying is finished, the land has to be restored to its original appearance. This can be very expensive. It may also be difficult to get plants to grow as quarries are often short of water and soil. Sketch **D** shows a method used in the Lake District. The quarry is filled with household waste, the ground is made level, topsoil is added and then trees are planted.

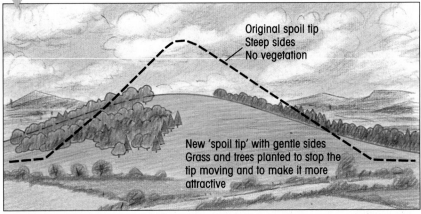

B

Original spoil tip
Steep sides
No vegetation

New 'spoil tip' with gentle sides
Grass and trees planted to stop the tip moving and to make it more attractive

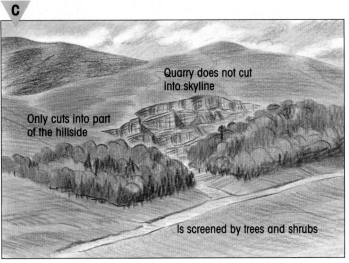

C

Quarry does not cut into skyline

Only cuts into part of the hillside

Is screened by trees and shrubs

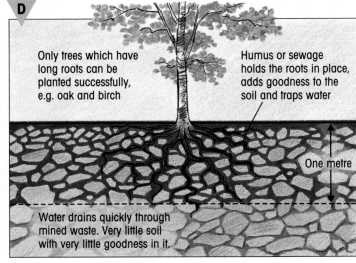

D

Only trees which have long roots can be planted successfully, e.g. oak and birch

Humus or sewage holds the roots in place, adds goodness to the soil and traps water

One metre

Water drains quickly through mined waste. Very little soil with very little goodness in it.

Sketch **F** shows a restored quarry near the Roman Wall in Northumberland National Park. The quarry was used until 1978. When it closed it left a hole 30 metres deep and the size of 16 hockey or football pitches. The hole was flooded and was dangerous. The quarry also had many old, unused buildings and piles of mined waste.

Some of the ways in which the quarry has been improved since then are shown on sketch **F**. Photo **E** shows how far the improvements had got by 1997.

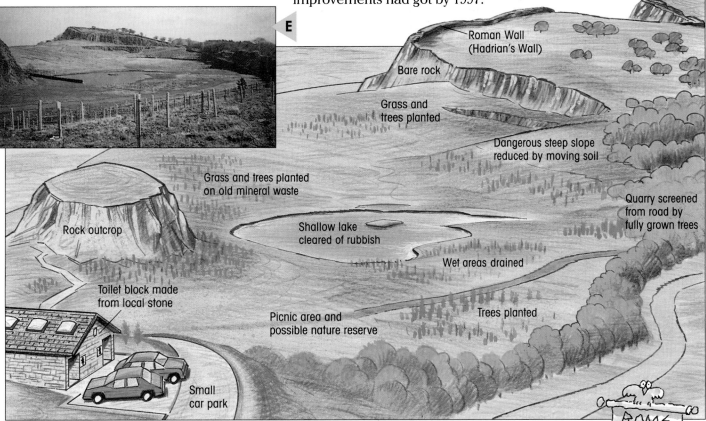

E

F

Roman Wall (Hadrian's Wall)

Bare rock

Grass and trees planted

Dangerous steep slope reduced by moving soil

Quarry screened from road by fully grown trees

Grass and trees planted on old mineral waste

Rock outcrop

Shallow lake cleared of rubbish

Wet areas drained

Toilet block made from local stone

Picnic area and possible nature reserve

Trees planted

Small car park

ROME RULES OK!

It's changed a lot since I was last here!

Activities

1 Choose **either** a gravel pit **or** a spoil tip. It can either be one of those shown on page 22 or one near to where you live.
   a) Say if it is a gravel pit or a spoil tip.
   b) Explain how it used to spoil the scenery and was dangerous to people.
   c) Describe how it has been made more attractive and less dangerous.

2 Look at sketch **F** and photo **E**.
   a) In 1978 a 'Warning – keep out' notice was put up in the quarry. Draw the notice and add what might have been written on it.
   b) How had the changes made to the quarry by 1997 improved the landscape for
   ● people
   ● wildlife?

3 You and your family decide to visit the quarry for a half a day. Describe what each member of your family might do during your visit.

WARNING KEEP OUT

Summary

Attempts are now being made to improve landscapes which have been damaged by mining and quarrying. These improvements may cost a lot of money and take a long time.

What factors influence farming?

Farming, or **agriculture**, is the growing of crops and raising of animals. Farming has changed the natural landscape in many parts of the world. There are three main types of farming:

- **Arable** is the ploughing of land and the growing of crops.

- **Pastoral** is leaving the land under grass for the grazing of animals.
- **Mixed farming** is when crops and animals are found in the same area.

B Pastoral farming

A Arable farming

Farming, especially in Britain, is big business. Farmers must carefully choose the best type of farming for the place where they farm. Deciding which is the best type depends upon several physical and human factors (sketches **C**, **D** and **E**).

Physical factors influencing farming

C

We grow fruit and other crops. They need a lot of sun to ripen them.

Climate is very important

My cows need grass. Grass is best if there is a lot of rain.

My crops need some rain, but not too much.

It has to be warm enough for several months for the fruit and crops to ripen.

D

Relief and **soils** are also very important

I grow crops in lowland areas. Here the relief is low and the slopes are usually gentle. The soil is often deep and has a lot of goodness in it.

I look after sheep in hilly areas. Here the relief is high and the slopes are often steep. The soil is usually thin and has little goodness in it.

E Human factors influencing farming

Size ...

Some farms are **very large**. This is where **either**
- farmers need a lot of land on which to grow crops or raise animals

or
- where there are only a few farmers in a large area.

Some farms are **very small**. This is where **either**
- farmers only need a little land to support their families

or
- there are lots of farmers working in a small area.

Farmers have been helped in some parts of the world by improved **transport**. In Britain dairy farmers have been helped by special milk lorries which keep the milk fresh on the journey to market. Better roads and motorways get the milk to markets more quickly.

... technology, transport and markets

The **technology** (machinery) available to farmers is also important. In Britain most farmers use modern machines to help them with their work. In poorer countries most of the work on a farm has to be done by hand.

What a farm produces may also depend on its distance from the **market**. The market is where farmers sell their produce. Farmers who grow crops that are heavy (e.g. potatoes) or soon go bad (e.g. strawberries) must be near to the market.

Activities

1 Match the following beginnings to the correct endings.

Arable farming	is rearing animals
Pastoral farming	is rearing animals and growing crops
Mixed farming	is growing crops

2 Diagram **F** shows some newspaper headlines about problems which affect farming. Draw table **G** below and sort the headlines into the correct columns.

F

Farms too small for family to earn a living

Ferry strike – fruit rots in French ports

High electricity prices – dairy farmers with milk machines hit hard

Crops ruined by flooding

Sheep are stranded in snowdrifts

Wet summers cause disease in potatoes

Fruit blossoms killed by frost

Rise in petrol prices

Daffodils flattened by strong winds

G

Problems which affect farming	
Physical	Human

E X T R A

If there is a farm near you:
- Is it mainly an arable, a pastoral or a mixed farm?
- How have physical factors influenced the farmer?
- How have human factors influenced the farmer?

Summary

Farming is influenced by physical and human factors. Physical factors are climate, relief and soils. Human factors include farm size, technology, distance from markets, and transport.

Farming where physical influences are more important

The River Ganges is found in northern India. The land through which it flows is one of the most crowded places in the world (page 68). Most of the people who live here are **subsistence** rice farmers. Subsistence farming is when, despite a lot of hard work, farmers only produce enough for their own needs and have little extra for sale.

Successful rice harvests in the Ganges Valley depend upon local physical conditions. Temperatures are high enough for crops to be grown throughout the year (graph **A**). Two crops can be harvested from the same field each year. Rainfall is the big problem. India has a **monsoon** climate. This means that for part of the year there is very heavy rain and for the remainder there is very little (graph **A**). Heavy rain is needed to flood the fields so that rice can be planted (photo **B**). Too little rain means that the harvest will be poor and farmers may be short of food. Too much rain can cause severe flooding which may destroy the crop. In the dry season (photo **C**) there is not enough water for rice to grow.

The land on both sides of the river is very flat and floods most years. Flooding provides water and leaves a layer of very fertile soil called **silt** (see page 13).

A The Ganges Valley

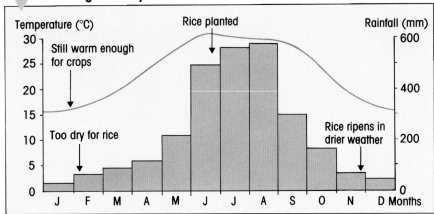

Temperature (°C)
Rainfall (mm)

Rice planted

Still warm enough for crops

Too dry for rice

Rice ripens in drier weather

J F M A M J J A S O N D Months

B

D

C

Rice farming is **labour-intensive**. This means it needs a large number of people to work on a small area of land. Many farms are only the size of a football pitch. Few farmers can afford machines and so work is done by hand or with the help of water buffalo (photo **D**). With little spare food to sell it hardly matters that local transport is poor, and the nearest market may be a long way from the farm.

Farming where human influences are more important

The San Joaquin Valley is found in California in the USA. The valley is not very crowded and most of the people who live here are **commercial** fruit and vegetable farmers. Commercial farming is when most of the produce is sold for profit.

Although temperatures in California are lower than those in India, they are high enough for some crops to be grown throughout the year. The biggest problem is water supply. Although both the San Joaquin and Ganges Valleys have long dry seasons, in California this comes in summer just when crops need most water (graph **E**). The fertile valley soils have to be artificially watered (**irrigated**). Unfortunately the water soon evaporates leaving the soil salty. Crops cannot grow in salty soil.

Successful **market gardening** (fruit and vegetable growing) depends mainly on the use of high technology and large amounts of money. The north of California gets plenty of rain and very few people live there. Large, expensive dams have been built to store water and to produce hydro-electricity (map **F**). The electricity is used to pump water along a series of canals to the drier, more populated parts of southern California. Smaller drainage channels, sprinklers and sprays are then used to water cotton, vines, fruit and vegetables (photo **G**).

Using money and technology the San Joaquin farmers, with their large farms, have many labour-saving machines for planting, weeding and harvesting crops.

E The San Joaquin Valley

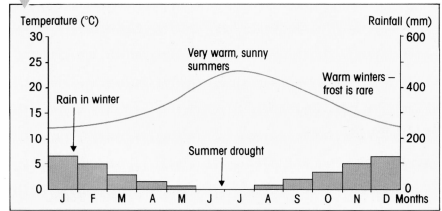

Mexican workers provide cheap labour at harvest time (page 74). Once harvested, the crops can be sent quickly, by lorry, along modern highways (motorways), or by rail to large urban markets. San Francisco and Los Angeles are the biggest markets.

F Water and electricity in California

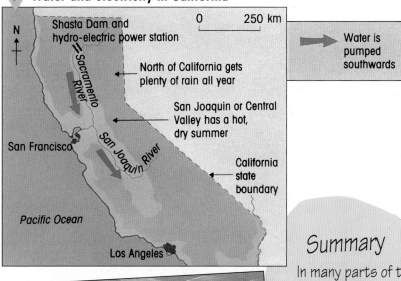

G

Irrigation in the San Joaquin Valley

Summary

In many parts of the world physical influences are more important than human influences. Sometimes, with money and technology, physical difficulties can be reduced.

Activities

1 Draw two star diagrams showing farming in the Ganges Valley. Add physical influences to the first and human influences to the second.

2 Repeat the activity for farming in the San Joaquin Valley.

Why do farms differ in size and land use?

Where farms are small, farmers must either employ many workers (**labour**) or spend a lot of money (**capital**) if they are to feed themselves or earn a living. These farmers must make the greatest possible use of every piece of land. This is called **intensive farming**.

In other parts of the world farms are much larger. Where there are fewer farmers living in an area or where more land is needed to earn a living, farms extend over a bigger area. This is called **extensive farming**.

A

An intensive farm in Lincolnshire

◆ Lincolnshire is a county in eastern England.

◆ Summers here are warm and sunny, winters are cold. Rainfall is fairly light.

◆ Much of the land is flat and the soil is deep. It is a good area for market gardening and many farms specialise in growing fruit, vegetables and flowers.

◆ The farm is very expensive to run and so the maximum use has to be made of the land. For each hectare the farmer gets either 2,500 boxes of celery, 35 tonnes of potatoes or 35 tonnes of sugar beet. A hectare is about the size of a football pitch.

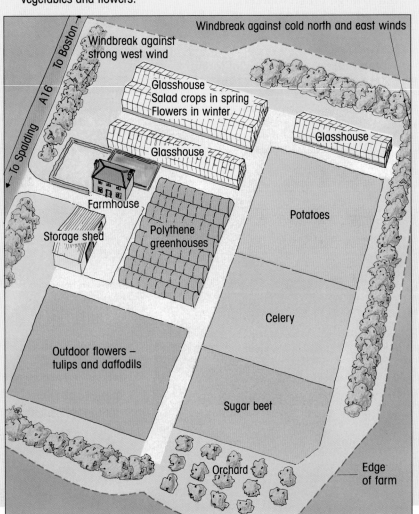

To Boston
To Spalding
A16

Windbreak against strong west wind

Windbreak against cold north and east winds

Glasshouse
Salad crops in spring
Flowers in winter

Glasshouse

Glasshouse

Farmhouse

Storage shed

Polythene greenhouses

Potatoes

Celery

Outdoor flowers – tulips and daffodils

Sugar beet

Orchard

Edge of farm

Farm size	20 hectares
Field size (average)	3 hectares
Workers	3 full-time and 7 seasonal
Animals	None
Crops	Flowers, lettuce, tomatoes, potatoes, celery and sugar beet
Machinery	2 tractors, sugar beet harvester, potato planter and harvester, sprayer, forklift truck, etc.
Special buildings	Movable polythene greenhouses Fixed glasshouses with central heating and sprinklers Computers control heat, moisture and ventilation Plants can be grown all year round
Fertiliser	Much expensive artificial fertiliser

B

An extensive farm in the Lake District

◆ The Lake District is in north-west England.

◆ In upland areas summers are cool, winters are cold and rainfall is heavy.

◆ The land is high and steep, and soils are thin and poor in quality.

◆ Sheep are reared on the hills and some cattle in the valleys.

◆ It takes a lot of land to provide enough grass to feed the sheep. Notice how the land use changes from the lakeside to the hilltop.

High fell – poor grazing on unfenced land, including rough pasture, peat moors and rock

Allotment – rough pasture in large fields surrounded by stone walls

Inbye – good grazing on flatter land near to the farmhouse and lake

Metres above sea level

Windy, colder, 2,500 mm rainfall per year

Sheltered, warmer by 5°C, 1,000 mm rainfall per year

Road
Lake
Inbye
Inbye
Farm
Inbye
Inbye
Inbye
Allotment
Allotment
500
400
300
200

Farm size	1,000 hectares
Field size (average)	5 hectares near lake. No fields higher up
Workers	3 full-time
Animals	3,000 sheep and lambs, 34 young beef cattle, 30 chickens, 3 sheepdogs
Crops	Grass for hay and silage, turnips
Machinery	Silage cutter
Special buildings	Lambing shed
Fertiliser	Natural manure

Activities

1 Copy out the paragraphs in the box below, choosing the correct word from each pair given in the brackets.

Intensive farming is making the (least/most) use of the land. It needs either (few/many) workers or (little/much) money. In Britain one area where intensive farming takes place is (the Lake District/Lincolnshire).

Extensive farming is using (large/small) amounts of land. It needs relatively (few/many) workers and (little/much) money. In Britain one area where extensive farming takes place is (the Lake District/Lincolnshire).

2 There are many differences between a Lake District and a Lincolnshire farm. Using the information on these two pages, describe, and try to give reasons for, the differences in:
a) farm size
b) field size
c) workers
d) animals
e) crops grown
f) machinery
g) special buildings
h) type of fertiliser.

Summary

Farms can differ in size and land use. Crops are usually grown on small farms where the greatest use has to be made of the land. Animals are more likely to be found on farms with large amounts of land.

How has farming changed the landscape?

Most of southern Britain was once covered in forest and marshland. As farming developed the forests were cleared and the marshes were drained. Later, hedges were planted and stone walls built. These created the fields which we now think of as being typical of farming areas.

Recently many more changes have taken place in our landscape. Sketch **A** shows some of the changes which have taken place in the last 50 years.

A

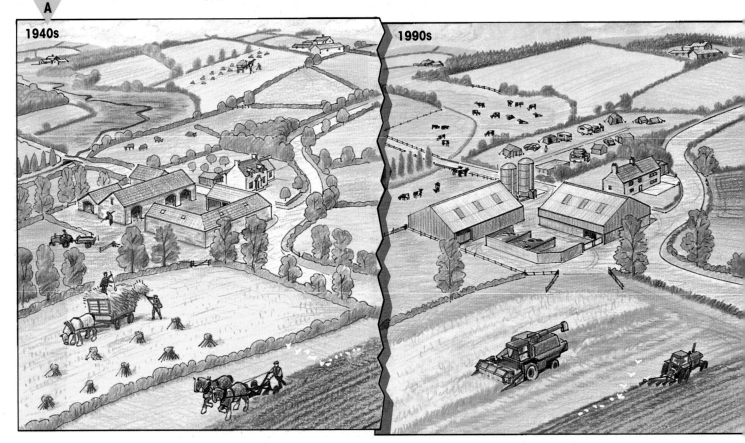

1940s
1990s

It is the farmers' job to try to produce more of our food. To do so they have drained **wetlands** and cleared **hedgerows**. These two changes have upset many people.

Wetlands are marshy areas. They also form one of the last of our natural environments, providing homes for a wide variety of

wildlife. As wetlands are drained, mainly for pastoral farming, the habitats of many birds, insects, animals and plants are destroyed.

Hedges were planted to stop animals from wandering and to show boundaries of land. Many people consider hedges to be very important to the environment. While farmers may share these views, it is their land which is taken up by hedges and their job to look after them. Since 1945, about one kilometre of hedge out of every four has been cleared (diagram **B**). Every cleared kilometre gives one extra hectare of land. (Remember some farms in India are only that size!)

B

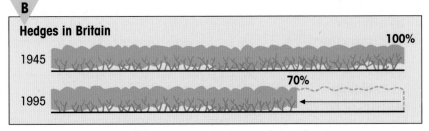

Hedges in Britain

1945	100%
1995	70%

C Advantages and disadvantages of hedges

Well looked after hedges are attractive

Hedge roots hold the soil together and reduce erosion

Hedges provide a home for wildlife

Cutting hedges costs the farmer time and money. A hedgecutter costs over £7,000

Hedges take up space which could be used for farmland

Hedges get in the way of big machinery in fields

D

Photo **D** shows soil erosion in central England. This happens when soil is no longer protected by the hedges. In this case it is blown away by very strong winds.

E X T R A

Activities

1 **Spot the differences** in the two sketches in **A**. Try to find one difference for each of the following: *field size, farm buildings, machinery, hedgerows, wetlands.*

2 Find a partner in your class. One of you will be a farmer, the other will be a conservationist.
  a) If you are the farmer, say:
  ● why you planted hedges in the first place
  ● why you now wish to remove them.

  b) If you are the conservationist, explain why you feel it is very important to keep the hedges.
  Both of you should get help from photo **C**.

Find out what is meant by **soil erosion**. Why are parts of eastern England affected by soil erosion when it is very windy? Apart from losing it by wind, how else may farmers lose their soil?

Summary

The present appearance of much of Britain's landscape is the result of farming. As farming changes, then so too does our landscape.

What is the distribution pattern of farming in Britain?

We have seen how the type and methods of farming are influenced by physical and human factors. As these factors can change within a few kilometres, so too can the type of farming. To draw a detailed and accurate map to show where the main farming types are found in Britain would be very complicated. It is often more meaningful to draw a simplified, or generalised, map instead.

Map **A** is generalised. It is easy to draw and to understand. However, if you look at an atlas map showing 'farming in Britain' you will see several important differences which the generalised map cannot show. These include arable farming in eastern Scotland, sheep on the Pennines and market gardening in Lancashire.

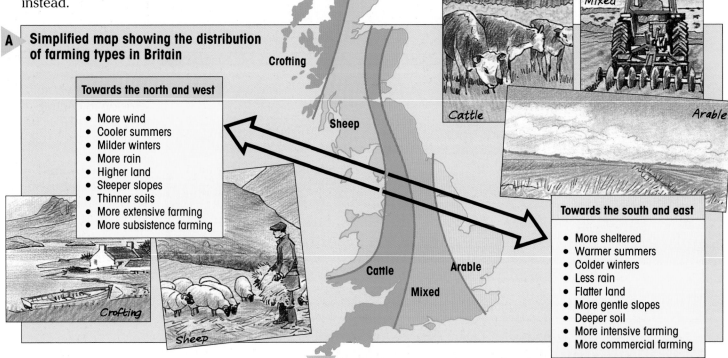

A Simplified map showing the distribution of farming types in Britain

Crofting

Towards the north and west

- More wind
- Cooler summers
- Milder winters
- More rain
- Higher land
- Steeper slopes
- Thinner soils
- More extensive farming
- More subsistence farming

Sheep

Mixed

Cattle

Arable

Towards the south and east

- More sheltered
- Warmer summers
- Colder winters
- Less rain
- Flatter land
- More gentle slopes
- Deeper soil
- More intensive farming
- More commercial farming

Cattle   **Arable**

Mixed

Crofting

Sheep

How is this distribution pattern changing?

The most recent changes have resulted from decisions made by the European Union (the EU) in Brussels. For example, since the mid-1970s there has been a rapid increase in farm cultivation of **oilseed rape** in Britain (photo **B**). This crop is grown for several reasons:

- Britain and the EU are short of oilseed.
- Oilseed is used to make margarine and cooking oil. By producing our own oil, shop prices are kept lower.
- Farmers get a high price for oilseed.
- After harvesting, the remains can be fed to cattle.
- Rape puts goodness (nitrogen) back into the soil and so is an ideal rotation crop.

B

Although some parts of the world are short of food, Britain and the EU have been producing too much. When too much food is produced it is called a **surplus**. This surplus food is not sold to poorer countries but is stored. Stores of food like butter, wheat and beef are called **food mountains**. Reserves of liquids like milk, wine and olive oil are called **food lakes**. To try to get rid of these 'mountains' and 'lakes' the EU has reduced money paid to farmers (**subsidies**). Farmers are now paid money to use their land in other ways. Two of these are shown in diagrams **C** and **D**.

C

Set-aside land
£200 per hectare per year is given to arable farmers if they stop growing crops for five years on over 20% of their land. The land can be left under grass, sold as building land or turned into woodland. Most farmers who have accepted this offer are leaving their land under grass (fallow).

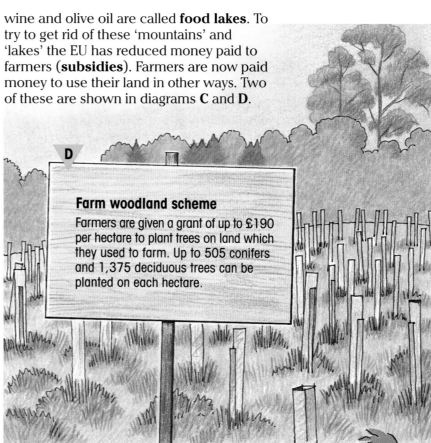

D

Farm woodland scheme
Farmers are given a grant of up to £190 per hectare to plant trees on land which they used to farm. Up to 505 conifers and 1,375 deciduous trees can be planted on each hectare.

Activities

1 Five types of farming are shown on map **A**. Match each type with the following five descriptions.
   ● Animals kept for milk and meat
   ● A subsistence form of farming
   ● Growing crops
   ● Growing crops and rearing animals
   ● Hill farming

2 **a)** What is oilseed rape?
   b) Give four reasons why it has become an important crop in Britain.

E X T R A

You are an arable farmer. The EU decides to give you less money for your crops. Would you:
   ■ still go on growing crops
   ■ 'set-aside' some land as grass (fallow) or
   ■ plant several hectares of trees?
Give reasons for your decision.

3 Diagram **E** shows food surpluses as 'mountains' and 'lakes'.
   a) What is a food surplus?
   b) Draw the diagram and then label:
   ● three products which make 'mountains'
   ● three products which form 'lakes'.

E

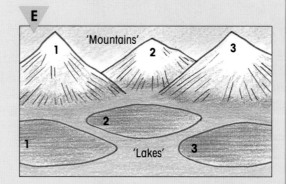

Summary

It is possible to recognise a generalised distribution pattern of farming in Britain. This pattern has taken centuries to develop and is still changing.

3 Secondary activities

What are secondary activities?

We have already seen that primary industry makes up one group of economic activities (page 20). **Primary industries** are those economic activities that collect or produce natural resources obtained from the land or sea. A second group of economic activities are **secondary industries**. This is when people make things from natural resources. Another name for these industries is **manufacturing**. Manufacturing usually takes place in **factories**. Secondary industry also includes putting together (**assembling** and **constructing**) manufactured goods. Four examples of secondary activities are shown in **A**, **B**, **C** and **D**.

A third group of economic activities are the **tertiary industries**. These provide a service, such as selling the manufactured goods.

A

It used to take a lot of people to work the machines.

B

A modern factory where people need a lot of skill.

C

A modern car assembly plant where very few people are needed to work the machines.

D

This shows the construction (building) industry.

34

Why do factories differ in size?

Different types of secondary activity take up different amounts of land. Photo **E** shows a steelworks in South Wales. Under the photo are some of the reasons why it takes up so much space.

Photo **F** is a small factory near to the centre of a large city. Above this photo are reasons why it only uses a small amount of space.

E

- ◆ Uses a main road
- ◆ Does not need to store many raw materials
- ◆ Produces small amounts of various goods
- ◆ Uses very few, small machines
- ◆ Very few people work here

F

- ◆ Has its own roads and railways
- ◆ Needs to store large amounts of raw materials
- ◆ Produces lots of steel
- ◆ Uses many large machines
- ◆ Many people work here

Activities

1 Find the following ten words in the wordsearch and then put them into the correct column in the table below.

| bread | coal | fish | furniture | ships |
| slate | steel | textiles | trees | wheat |

Clue: five words are natural resources and five are manufactured goods.

```
H W M N S H I P S
S L A T E B Y P C
I D O Z L Q U B V
F U R N I T U R E
F C G K T R E E S
L O H K X T L A Y
J A W H E A T D E
D L E E T S S I F
```

Natural resources	Manufactured goods

2 Write down the difference between a natural resource and a manufactured item.

E X T R A

Copy out and complete the table below. In the first column list several factories found in your home area. For each factory say what it makes, how big it is and give a reason for its size.

Factory	What it makes	Size (big or small)	Why it is big or small

Summary

Secondary industry (activity) is when natural resources are made into goods which can be used by people or other industries. Most secondary industry takes place in factories. Some factories need large amounts of land, while other factories take up very little space.

What is the best site for a factory?

Before building a factory a manufacturer should try to work out the best site for its location. It is unusual to find a perfect site for a factory. Indeed, if there was a perfect site someone else would probably already be using it. Deciding on the best available site depends on several things. Six of these are given in sketch **A**.

A

1 My factory uses lots of **raw materials**. It costs money and takes time to move them so it is best if my factory is as close as possible to these materials. This is even more important if the materials are big and heavy.

2 My factory needs lots of **power** (energy) to work the machines. When the factory was first built a fast flowing river powered the machines. Now we use electricity.

3 A few years ago many people (**labour**) were needed to work in my factory. Today a few machines can do most of this work. However, my present small labour force must be trained and skilled.

4 The best place for any factory is near to a large urban **market**. A market is where most of the people who buy the goods live.

5 **Transport** was a very important factor in choosing the site for my factory. It is needed to bring raw materials and workers to the factory and to send manufactured goods to the market.

6 The **site** for the factory is good because there is plenty of cheap flat land there.

Textiles are often the first industry to be developed in a country. In Britain the first two important textile areas were in East Anglia and the Cotswolds. Later the industry moved to Yorkshire and Lancashire because these areas had more advantages. Yorkshire became important for woollen textiles and Lancashire for cotton textiles. Sketch **B** shows why parts of Yorkshire gave the best location for woollen mills (factories).

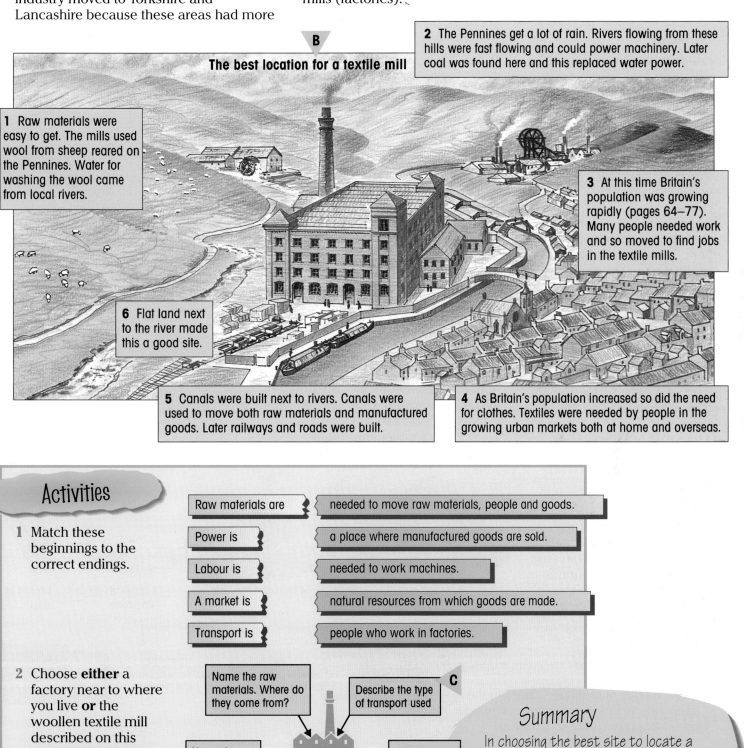

B

The best location for a textile mill

2 The Pennines get a lot of rain. Rivers flowing from these hills were fast flowing and could power machinery. Later coal was found here and this replaced water power.

1 Raw materials were easy to get. The mills used wool from sheep reared on the Pennines. Water for washing the wool came from local rivers.

3 At this time Britain's population was growing rapidly (pages 64–77). Many people needed work and so moved to find jobs in the textile mills.

6 Flat land next to the river made this a good site.

5 Canals were built next to rivers. Canals were used to move both raw materials and manufactured goods. Later railways and roads were built.

4 As Britain's population increased so did the need for clothes. Textiles were needed by people in the growing urban markets both at home and overseas.

Activities

1 Match these beginnings to the correct endings.

Raw materials are	needed to move raw materials, people and goods.
Power is	a place where manufactured goods are sold.
Labour is	needed to work machines.
A market is	natural resources from which goods are made.
Transport is	people who work in factories.

2 Choose **either** a factory near to where you live **or** the woollen textile mill described on this page. Using diagram **C** as a guide, explain why the factory or mill grew at that site.

C

Name the raw materials. Where do they come from?

Describe the type of transport used

Name the type of power

Mill or factory

Where are the markets?

Describe the land at the site

Where do the workers come from? Are many needed?

Summary

In choosing the best site to locate a factory, a manufacturer should consider transport and the nearness to raw materials, power sources, workers, and markets for its goods.

Choosing the right site

Industries near to raw materials

Britain was the first country in the world to become **industrialised**. Industrialisation began about 200 years ago after the discovery that coal could be used to produce steam and that steam could be used to work machines. Machines did many of the jobs previously done by people.

In those days transport was poor. There were no lorries or trains, no motorways or railways. Coal and other raw materials were heavy and expensive to move. This meant that most early industries grew up on Britain's coalfields (map **A**). The most important industry became the production of iron and, after 1856, steel.

The iron and steel industry

Three raw materials are needed to make iron and steel – iron ore, coal and, in smaller amounts, limestone. Coke, from coal, is used to **smelt** (melt) the iron ore. This is done because iron ore contains impurities such as carbon. Limestone is added to help separate the pure

iron from the impurities leaving steel behind. Diagram **B** shows what was needed to make one tonne of steel in the nineteenth century.

This meant that early iron works were located on coalfields where iron ore was found nearby (map **A**).

When steel was made instead of iron, steelworks still favoured coalfield locations. Steel was used to make things like ships, trains, bridges and textile machinery. As these industries grew in size and number, many people moved to them to find work. Most coalfields became crowded with people. Today many of these early industrial areas have used up their raw materials. Their industries are in decline, factories have closed, it is hard for people to find jobs, and the environment has often been left spoilt.

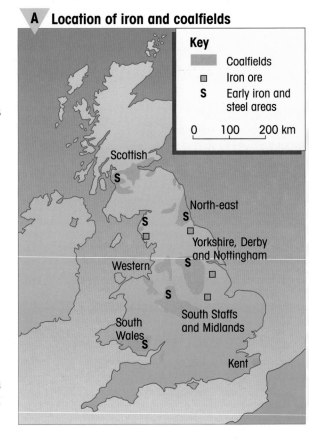

A Location of iron and coalfields

Key
- Coalfields
- Iron ore
- **S** Early iron and steel areas

0   100   200 km

Scottish

North-east

Yorkshire, Derby and Nottingham

Western

South Staffs and Midlands

South Wales

Kent

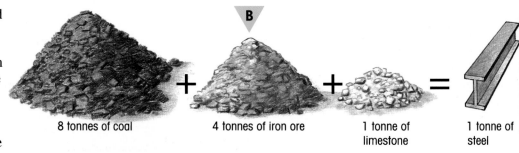

B

8 tonnes of coal   +   4 tonnes of iron ore   +   1 tonne of limestone   =   1 tonne of steel

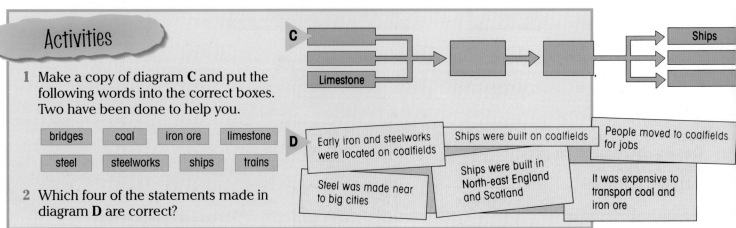

Activities

1 Make a copy of diagram **C** and put the following words into the correct boxes. Two have been done to help you.

| bridges | coal | iron ore | limestone |

| steel | steelworks | ships | trains |

C

Limestone

Ships

2 Which four of the statements made in diagram **D** are correct?

D

Early iron and steelworks were located on coalfields

Ships were built on coalfields

People moved to coalfields for jobs

Steel was made near to big cities

Ships were built in North-east England and Scotland

It was expensive to transport coal and iron ore

Industries near to markets

As raw materials are used up, and as transport improves, then modern factories tend to locate in areas where many people live. This is mainly because present day industries need large markets in which to sell their goods. The car industry is an example of an industry which is building new factories near to markets.

The car industry

A modern car consists of many small parts. Each part will be made in its own factory. If the factories making these parts are all close together then it will be easier and cheaper for the car manufacturer to **assemble** (put together) all of these parts. If large towns are nearby then workers from these towns can make and assemble the parts and, hopefully, buy many of the finished cars. Transport is important for moving car parts, assembled cars and workers. Map **E** shows where most people in Britain live and where the largest car assembly plants are located.

Today industrial growth is more likely in those areas where there are most people. In these places new factories are opening, jobs are easier to get, and more care is taken of the environment.

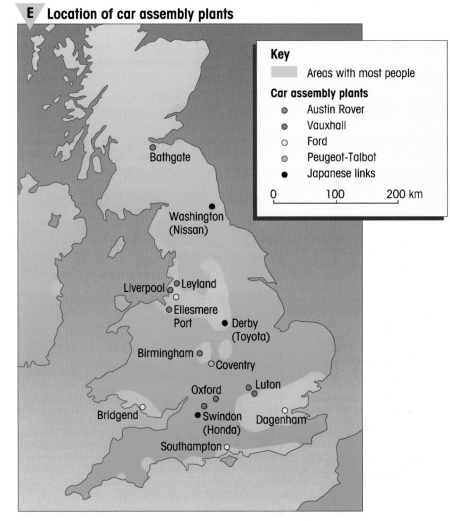

E Location of car assembly plants

Key
- Areas with most people

Car assembly plants
- Austin Rover
- Vauxhall
- Ford
- Peugeot-Talbot
- Japanese links

0   100   200 km

Bathgate
Washington (Nissan)
Liverpool · Leyland
Ellesmere Port · Derby (Toyota)
Birmingham · Coventry
Oxford · Luton
Bridgend · Swindon (Honda) · Dagenham
Southampton

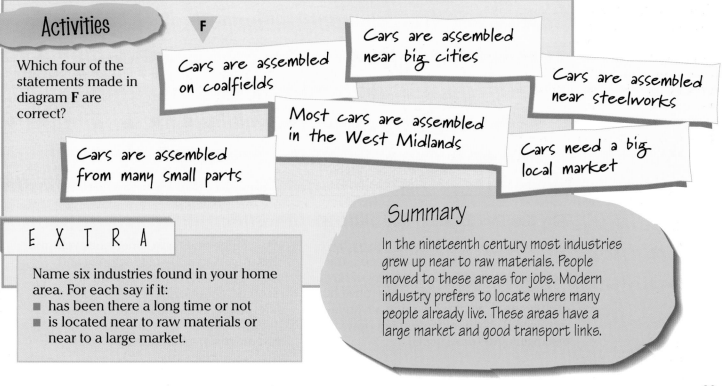

Activities

F

Which four of the statements made in diagram **F** are correct?

Cars are assembled on coalfields

Cars are assembled near big cities

Cars are assembled near steelworks

Most cars are assembled in the West Midlands

Cars are assembled from many small parts

Cars need a big local market

EXTRA

Name six industries found in your home area. For each say if it:
- has been there a long time or not
- is located near to raw materials or near to a large market.

Summary

In the nineteenth century most industries grew up near to raw materials. People moved to these areas for jobs. Modern industry prefers to locate where many people already live. These areas have a large market and good transport links.

Industries in the inner city

Before industrialisation began in Britain, many towns in Wales, Scotland and the north of England were small. As industry grew so did the need for workers. When the workers moved to the towns to find jobs they needed houses in which to live. At that time there were no private cars or buses so people had to walk to work. It was best for them if they lived near to the factory or mill in which they worked (photo **A**). So in the early nineteenth century both industry and terraced housing grew up on what were then the edges of towns. Since then towns have continued to grow. Those early industries and houses have been surrounded by newer buildings, leaving them in what we now call the 'inner city'.

Until recently most industries were still located in the inner cities. Indeed, as drawing **B** shows, there were still several good points to those industries having a location there.

A

B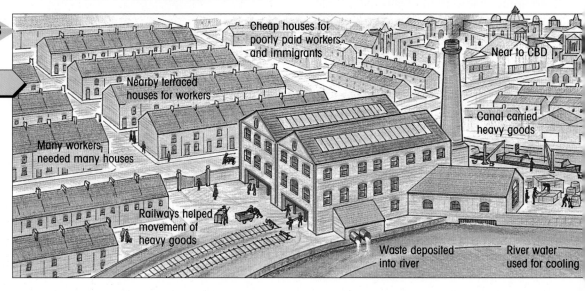

Cheap houses for poorly paid workers and immigrants

Near to CBD

Early good points

Nearby terraced houses for workers

Canal carried heavy goods

Many workers needed many houses

Railways helped movement of heavy goods

Waste deposited into river

River water used for cooling

Why has this location and pattern changed?

The needs of people and of industry have changed since the growth of those early factories. Many of the advantages of having a location near to the city centre have now disappeared. What were once advantages (drawing **B**) have now often become disadvantages (drawing **C**).

Many inner cities have been **redeveloped**. This means that the old factories and houses have been pulled down and replaced either by new buildings or by a different type of land use (drawing **D**). Modern industry now finds that it has more advantages in locating on the edges of towns and cities (page 42).

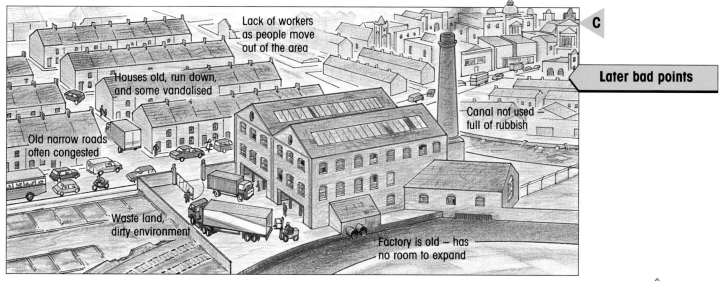

Lack of workers as people move out of the area

Houses old, run down, and some vandalised

Old narrow roads often congested

Waste land, dirty environment

Canal not used – full of rubbish

Factory is old – has no room to expand

C

Later bad points

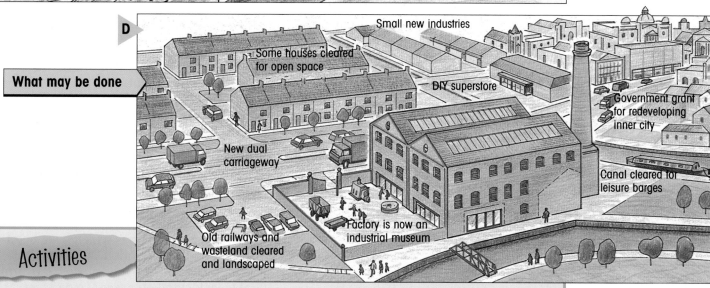

Small new industries

Some houses cleared for open space

DIY superstore

Government grant for redeveloping inner city

D

What may be done

New dual carriageway

Canal cleared for leisure barges

Old railways and wasteland cleared and landscaped

Factory is now an industrial museum

Activities

1 Eight points are made in diagram **E** about the location of a factory in an inner city area.

a) List four points which were important when the factory was first built.

b) List four points which show present day problems for a factory located in an inner city area.

Drawings **B** and **C** will help you with your answer.

E

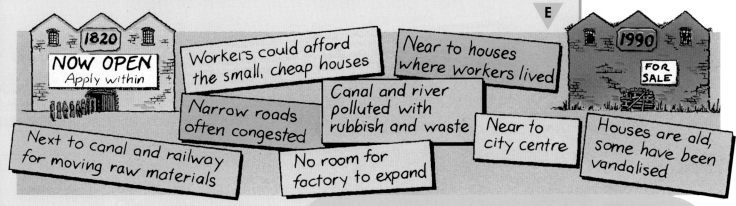

1820

NOW OPEN
Apply within

1990

FOR SALE

Workers could afford the small, cheap houses

Near to houses where workers lived

Canal and river polluted with rubbish and waste

Narrow roads often congested

Near to city centre

Houses are old, some have been vandalised

Next to canal and railway for moving raw materials

No room for factory to expand

2 Compare drawings **B** and **D**. List four ways in which land use in an inner city may have been changed over a period of time.

Summary

There were many advantages for early industry to locate in present day inner city areas. As many of these advantages no longer exist, the land use of inner cities is changing.

Why do industries group together?

We have already seen (page 39) that it is an advantage to the car industry if the many factories making individual car parts are located as close as possible to the assembly plant. Until recently the West Midlands was important for car assembly. Likewise, other places in Britain can be linked to a particular industry (diagram **A**).

However, if too many similar industries locate in the same place they might produce too many goods for people in the local area to buy. So there can also be disadvantages in industries seeking similar locations.

Information technology (IT) on science and business parks

Information technology, or **IT** for short, is when ideas and information are exchanged. At school you may have used a computer and a word processor, or seen a fax machine and weather satellite photos. At home your television might have teletext, while many shops use bar coding to check prices at their checkouts. All of these are examples of IT.

Information technology is a relatively new **high-tech** industry. Firms which make or use IT equipment often group together on pleasant, newly developed **science** or **business parks** (photo **B**). All firms on a science park are high-tech and have direct links with a university. Business parks do not have links with universities and may include superstores, hotels and leisure centres. There are many more business parks than there are science parks.

Both are located on edge-of-city **greenfield sites** although some business parks are found in inner city areas which have been redeveloped (e.g. London Docklands). Diagram **C** shows the advantages to IT firms that have located on a science park.

A

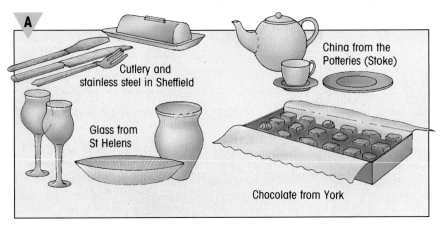

Cutlery and stainless steel in Sheffield

China from the Potteries (Stoke)

Glass from St Helens

Chocolate from York

B

Mature trees to screen buildings

Buildings have plenty of space

Large car parking areas

Modern buildings with central heating, air conditioning and large windows for light

Grassy areas, ornamental gardens, lakes and ponds

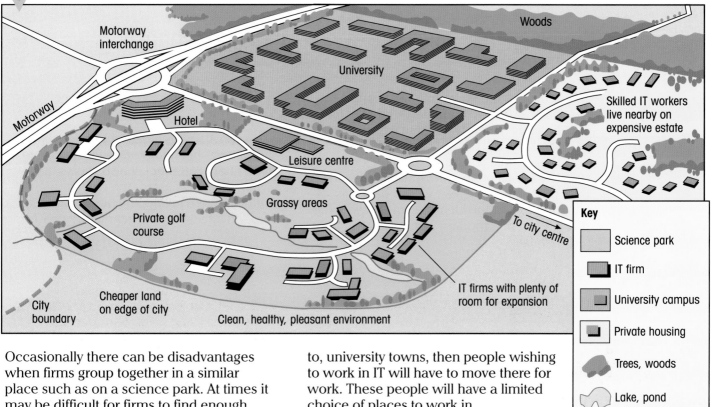

Key:
- Science park
- IT firm
- University campus
- Private housing
- Trees, woods
- Lake, pond

Labels on diagram: Motorway interchange, Woods, University, Skilled IT workers live nearby on expensive estate, Motorway, Hotel, Leisure centre, Grassy areas, Private golf course, To city centre, City boundary, Cheaper land on edge of city, Clean, healthy, pleasant environment, IT firms with plenty of room for expansion

Occasionally there can be disadvantages when firms group together in a similar place such as on a science park. At times it may be difficult for firms to find enough highly skilled workers. At other times firms may have to close down, leaving the town with an above average increase in unemployment.

How has IT affected where people work?
- As science parks are located in, or near to, university towns, then people wishing to work in IT will have to move there for work. These people will have a limited choice of places to work in.
- As science parks are located on the edges of cities then this reduces the number of jobs in the city centre.
- As information can be sent by fax, teletext and telephone then more people can work at home rather than in a factory or an office.

Activities

1 a) What is information technology (IT)?
   b) Give three ways in which you might use IT in a school-day.

2 Complete table **D** to show the differences between a science park and a business park. Choose your answers from the following pairs:
   a) many/very few
   b) university links/no university links
   c) high-tech firms/high-tech firms, shops, hotels and leisure centres.

3 Using photo **B** and diagram **C**, give **six** reasons why an IT firm should locate on a science park. In your answer you should mention each of the following: *transport, price of land, the environment, people's health, leisure facilities, exchanging ideas with people from other firms.*

4 Give two disadvantages which may arise from firms locating in the same place.

EXTRA

Name a science or business park in your home region. Describe its location, size and appearance. What types of firms are located on it?

D

	Science park	Business park
a		
b		
c		

Summary

There are advantages and disadvantages for firms that locate in the same place. IT firms often locate on edge-of-town science or business parks.

How can the ideal site for an industry change?

A factory should try to make a profit. We have already seen (page 36) that before building a factory a manufacturer should work out the best site to locate it. However, the advantages available when locating a textile mill or an iron works in the early 1800s may no longer exist today. This means that the ideal site for a new textile factory or a modern steelworks will have changed.

Changes in the iron and steel industry

Diagram **A** shows a part of Britain which has always been important for making iron and, after 1856, steel. It also shows that while the best sites for the early iron industry were inland, the best location for a modern steelworks is near to the coast.

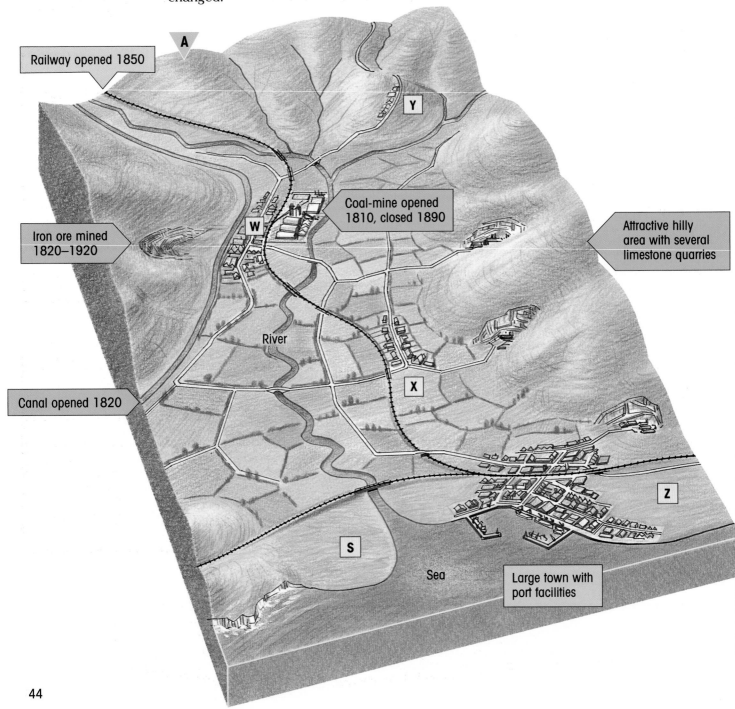

A

Railway opened 1850

Iron ore mined 1820–1920

Canal opened 1820

Coal-mine opened 1810, closed 1890

Attractive hilly area with several limestone quarries

River

Large town with port facilities

Sea

Y

W

X

Z

S

44

Activities

1 **In 1820** an iron manufacturer decided to build an ironworks in the area shown on diagram **A**. The manufacturer had to choose between sites **W**, **X**, **Y** and **Z**.

Some of the factors that had to be considered when choosing the site are listed in matrix **C**. The manufacturer eventually chose site **W** for the ironworks. To see why that site was chosen, try completing the matrix yourself.

a) Look carefully at diagram **A** and box **B**. For the first location factor give a score for each site. Do the same for each of the other location factors. Part of the matrix has been done to help you.

b) Add up the scores. The one with the highest total will be the best site. It should be site **W**. Give four reasons why **W** was a good site for an ironworks in 1820.

2 **By 1990** the factory at **W** no longer made a profit. It was too small and the coal and iron ore in the area had run out. These raw materials were now brought in from abroad by sea. It was decided that the factory had to be enlarged or a new steelworks built either at site **Z** or **S**.

Matrix **D** shows some of the factors that the manufacturer had to consider before deciding whether to stay at **W** or go to **Z** or **S**. You decide what should be done by completing the matrix. Remember that it is much cheaper to expand at the same place than to build a new factory at a different site.

a) Complete the matrix using the scoring from box **B**.

b) Did you decide to expand at **W** or did you choose one of the sites **Z** or **S**?

c) Write a short paragraph giving the reasons for your decision.

B

Give a score of 0 to 4 for each site.

4 if the site is **excellent**

3 if the site is **very good**

2 if the site is **good** but has faults

1 if the site is **poor** and only just acceptable

0 if the site is **unsatisfactory**

C

Location factors for ironworks in 1820	Site W	Site X	Site Y	Site Z
Near to local iron ore	4			1
Near to local coal		2		
Near to local limestone				
River or canal needed for transport	4			
Flat land needed for factory				4
Close to town for workers				
Total				

D

Location factors for steelworks in 1990	Site W	Site Z	Site S
Near to port for coal and iron imports			
Near to local limestone			
Railways and roads needed for transport			
Flat, cheap land needed for factory			
Near town for skilled workers			
Same or different location			
Total			

Summary The best site for an industry changes as location factors change. The British iron industry grew up near raw materials. Britain's few remaining steelworks are located near to the coast.

How can industry pollute the environment?

Industry has helped to make Britain one of the richer countries in the world. It makes goods which have improved our standard of living. But industry uses up **resources** (page 54), creates waste and can damage the environment.

In the past the main aim of industry was to make a profit. There was little concern or interest in the environment, especially as any damage caused by factories often affected only the local area. People in the main industrial towns of Britain just accepted smoke-filled skies, smoke-stained buildings, dirty rivers with no fish, and piles of coal and other industrial waste, as a normal part of their environment.

Today the effects of industry are so widespread that they are threatening the whole global environment.

A

Types of industrial pollution

Air

Smoke from chimneys can affect human health by causing breathing problems. Carbon dioxide in smoke is causing world temperatures to rise (see page 61). Other gases in smoke cause acid rain which kills trees and fish.

Water

Factories can allow waste materials to escape into rivers. Industries use water for cooling and return warm water to rivers. This can kill fish.

Visual

Few factories are attractive to look at. When factories close, the land may be left empty (derelict).

Some industries dump their waste materials. Sometimes this waste is dangerous, poisonous or radioactive.

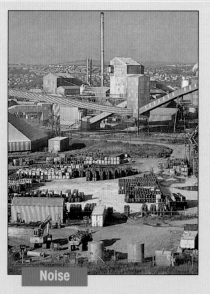

Noise

Lorries going to and from factories, and heavy machinery, create noise for people living nearby.

Smell

Some industries, such as the plastics industry, give off very unpleasant smells.

What can be done to reduce industrial pollution?

One way is by education. As more people become aware of the dangers of pollution, more pressure can be put on industry and governments to prevent further pollution. Results in the last few years have been more encouraging but it is impossible to solve all the problems at once. Likewise, it is impossible to clean up a polluted environment overnight.

A second way is to spend more money on preventing pollution. Unfortunately, not all industries and governments have the money, or the desire, to spend what little money they have on stopping pollution. Factories, and power stations producing energy for industry, can reduce the amount of smoke and gases they give out (page 61). However, this may mean a drop in profits or an increase in the price of goods.

Certainly there is an urgent need to plan and manage our environment more carefully (page 48). Prevention is easier than the cure!

Activities

1 Look at cartoon **B**.

B

a) Name the five types of pollution shown on the cartoon.

b) What two types of pollution would be the most damaging to plants and wildlife? Give reasons for your answer.

c) Imagine that you lived or worked in this area. Which two types of pollution would you dislike the most? Give reasons.

2 **a)** How can education help to reduce pollution?

b) Why do many industries not want to spend money on trying to reduce pollution?

3 When applied to pollution, what is meant by the term, 'prevention is easier than the cure'?

E X T R A

Work with a partner and produce a poster to show how industry pollutes the environment. Add a slogan to draw people's attention to these dangers.

Summary

Industry contributes towards air, water, noise, visual and smell pollution. Much education and money are needed to prevent pollution in the future. Cleaning up environments is costly, difficult, and may take a long time.

Why are we concerned about the environment?

The **environment** is everything around us. It includes the natural physical surroundings where people, plants and animals live.

Conservation of resources needs careful **planning and management**. Planning allows people to use resources to their best advantage without polluting the environment. Planning and management reduces conflict between groups of people and between people and the environment.

Planning means making decisions where there is a conflict of interest. For example, how can we build houses, create jobs and develop leisure activities while at the same time protecting the environment.

up!

Conservation of resources is very important. Conservation is the protection of resources for future use and limiting damage to the environment. This is known as **sustainable development**.

It is important to try to conserve the air, the sea, minerals, energy, soil, trees, wildlife and scenery.

Activities

1 **a)** Put these boxes in the correct order to explain why it is important to plan and manage the environment.
   b) Give an example for each box.

Resources are natural materials which are useful to people.

Pollution happens when people harm and destroy the environment.

Conservation is when people use resources carefully and protect the environment.

Planning and management is when people use resources without spoiling the environment.

The **environment** is the natural surroundings where people and animals live.

The environment contains **resources** which are materials that occur naturally. They are useful because they can improve people's lives.

Coal, iron ore, clean water, soil, trees, mountains, wildlife and sandy beaches are all examples of resources.

down!

People must use resources carefully. A careless use may mean that some resources will be **used up**, some will be **wasted**, and some may cause **pollution**. Pollution is when people harm or destroy the natural environment. Pollution can kill plants and animals.

People often misuse these resources. Some resources, like coal, are used up. Some, like forests and soil, are destroyed. Others, like rivers and the air, become polluted.

EXTRA

By yourself, as a group, or as a class, think of one way in which you can try to conserve and protect the environment. Try it out for one week. After the week
- decide if you were successful or not
- discuss with others why it is often hard to protect the environment.

2 Think about one normal day in your life. During the day you probably used up several resources, caused quite a lot of pollution and may have tried to conserve the environment.

Draw and complete a table like the one below to show, 'One day in my life'. Some ideas have been added to the table to help you.

Summary

If resources are misused they can be used up or they may harm the environment. It is important that resources are used sensibly and the environment is protected for the future. This needs careful planning and management.

Resources which I used up	Pollution which I caused	How I tried to conserve the environment
◆ Clean water	◆ Dirty water after my shower	◆ Went to the bottle-bank
◆ Had fish and chips at lunchtime	◆ Left chip paper in school playground	◆ Put empty drink can in dustbin

Who cares for the environment?

One of the jobs of the British Government is to try and protect the countryside. Three Government bodies are:

- the Countryside Commission which looks after country parks and long distance footpaths
- the Forestry Commission which is mainly interested in coniferous forests
- the Nature Conservancy Council which has developed Nature Reserves.

However, there are also many voluntary groups of people (**conservationists**) who are concerned with protecting the environment. Some of these groups are named in diagram **A**. All of these groups have to rely upon donations of money to help them do their job.

A

Each group tends to concentrate upon one, and sometimes more, aspects of the environment. Some look after areas of **attractive countryside**, some look after **wildlife habitats** while others are more interested in **historic sites** (diagram **B**). They are all working to stop further damage to the environment.

B

Areas of attractive countryside
- Rivers   ◆ Coasts
- Lakes   ◆ Moors
- Mountains

Wildlife habitats
(homes of plants and animals)
- Woods
- Hedges
- Wetlands (marshes)

Historic sites
- Stately homes
- Castles
- Industrial museums

Activities

1 What do we mean by the following terms?

conservationist

attractive countryside

wildlife habitat

historic site

areas of attractive countryside, wildlife habitats and historic sites. They have been numbered ① to ⑫.
a) Which three are likely to be looked after by Government bodies?
b) Which of the voluntary groups named in diagram A may look after each of the remaining nine environments?

2 Sketch C shows several different environments which need special protection. These environments are

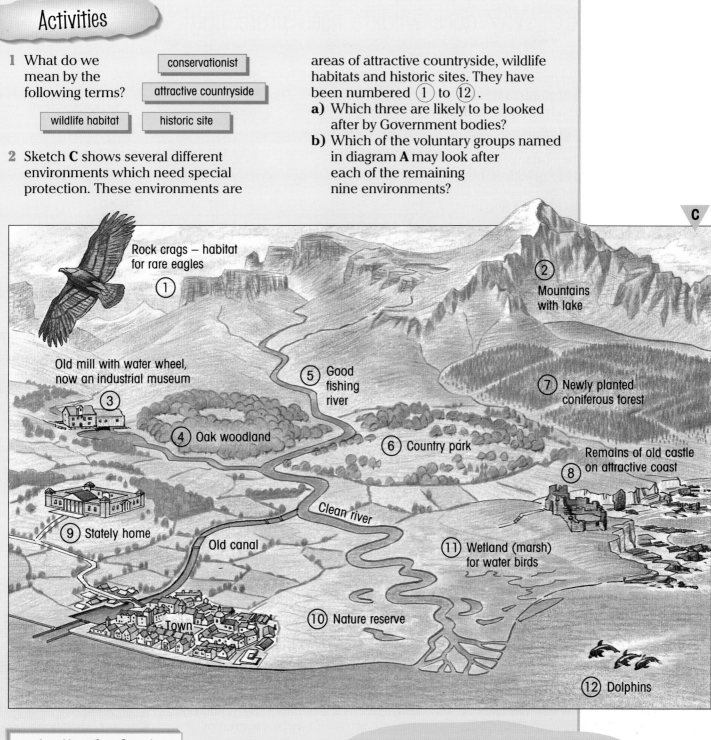

C

- ① Rock crags – habitat for rare eagles
- ② Mountains with lake
- ③ Old mill with water wheel, now an industrial museum
- ⑤ Good fishing river
- ⑦ Newly planted coniferous forest
- ④ Oak woodland
- ⑥ Country park
- ⑧ Remains of old castle on attractive coast
- Clean river
- ⑨ Stately home
- Old canal
- ⑪ Wetland (marsh) for water birds
- Town
- ⑩ Nature reserve
- ⑫ Dolphins

E X T R A

People in the town on sketch C like visiting the mountains and lake. They need a better road to make their journey easier and faster. Where would you build the road so that it did not upset any conservation group? Describe your route and say what problems there might be.

Summary

Some types of environment need special protection. These environments include areas of attractive countryside, wildlife habitats and historic sites. Some of these environments are looked after by Government bodies, while others are protected by voluntary conservation groups.

Why does wildlife need protecting?

Wildlife is always under threat from people. Some **species** (types) of plants, animals, birds and fish have already become **extinct**. Extinct means that there are no more of that species still living. Many other species of wildlife are said to be **endangered**. Unless something is done quickly to help and protect these endangered species they too will become extinct. Table **A** and the photos in **B** give examples of some endangered species, together with reasons why they have become endangered.

A

Examples of endangered species	Reasons for becoming endangered
Crocodiles and alligators	Skin is used for shoes, handbags and belts
Leopards, cheetahs and jaguars	Fur is used for clothes
Hawksbill turtles	Can no longer breed on beaches since these are full of tourists
Rhinos	Killed for their horns. A dagger with a rhino horn handle costs £10,000
Blue butterflies	Virtually extinct in the UK as their natural habitat has been destroyed
Whales and dolphins	Killed for food, caught in fishing nets
Elephants (photo **C**)	Killed for their ivory

Other endangered species include gorillas, giant pandas, tigers, parrots, orchids and many cacti plants.

B

Elephants in Kenya – the problem

The long tusks of elephants are made of ivory. Ivory is taken from dead elephants and many have been killed for their tusks. Their trunks are often cut off to make the job of hacking out the tusks with axes easier. Most of the ivory from Kenya was sent to places like Hong Kong and Japan to be made into ornaments (photo **D**). As the world's trade and the price of ivory increased, more and more elephants were killed. Even when the Kenyan Government created the country's first national park in 1948, it did not stop the many poachers from killing elephants. Of the 111,000 elephants in Kenya in 1973, only 65,000 were left by 1981 and 19,000 in 1987. In fourteen years more than eight out of every ten elephants were killed. The elephant had become an endangered species.

Kenya needs it elephants. They, and other animals, are an important source of wealth to the country because they attract tourists (photo **F**). Many people come from overseas to go on safari, which means they can see wildlife in its natural habitat. Elephants are also useful to other wildlife in the area. They dig for water in dry areas, making it available to other species, they make tracks for smaller animals through thick vegetation and, on death, provide food for many predators for many weeks.

What has been done?

- President Moi of Kenya, a keen conservationist, has done much to stop the world trade in ivory.
- Conservation groups like WWF (World Wide Fund for Nature) raised money to help guard the elephant. They helped set up a new conservation group called CITES (Convention on International Trade in Endangered Species). This led in 1990 to a world ban on trading in ivory.
- Education within Kenyan schools and advertising on T-shirts (cartoon **E**) has helped to protect elephants.

By the mid-1990s, the number of elephants, especially in southern Africa, had begun to increase. Some scientists and politicians now even suggest that elephants can be treated as a 'crop', and surplus elephants 'harvested'. Income from the sale of ivory, skins and meat could help local communities and pay for conservation.

IVORY SHOULD BE WORN ON ELEPHANTS NOT PEOPLE!

Activities

1   **a)** What is meant by 'endangered species'?
    b) Give **five** reasons why some species have become endangered.

2   Design **either** a poster **or** a T-shirt to remind people that ivory souvenirs will have cost an elephant its life.

3   Choose one endangered species. It might be one shown in the photos in **B** or another one that you know about. Explain why that species has become endangered. Give reasons why you think that it needs to be protected.

Summary

Many species of wildlife have become rare and are threatened with extinction. They need careful protection if they are to survive.

Why does the Antarctic need protecting?

The southern continent of Antarctica covers one tenth of the world's surface. Although larger than the continents of Europe and Australasia, it is a **wilderness**. It is called a wilderness because it is a desert of ice where nothing can grow and where nobody lives permanently. It is a place where the wind can reach 300 km per hour (190 m.p.h.), temperatures can fall below minus 50°C and the depth of ice can exceed 4,500 metres. Where the ice reaches the coast it forms tall ice cliffs. In time, huge blocks of ice break off to form icebergs (photo **A**).

Antarctica is the most unspoilt region on Earth. It is still mainly a natural environment free from pollution – but for how long? It is a continent with valuable resources – but how can it be protected?

A

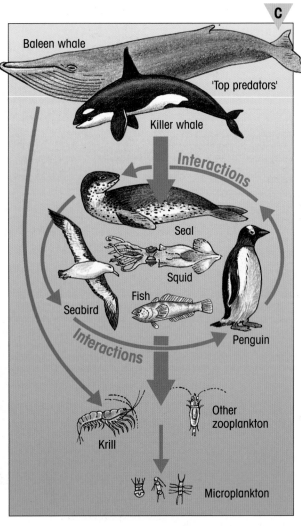
C

Baleen whale

'Top predators'

Killer whale

Interactions

Seal

Squid

Fish

Seabird

Penguin

Interactions

Krill

Other zooplankton

Microplankton

What are the Antarctic's resources?

B

The relatively few species of **wildlife** are, however, found in large numbers. All wildlife depends upon plankton and krill which thrive in the polar sea. Plankton is a minute plant which is eaten by the small shrimp-like krill. Krill provide the food for the majority of seabirds, fish, penguins, squid, seals and whales (photo **B** and diagram **C**). Several countries fish the Southern Ocean for krill, squid and fin fish. Although Antarctica contains mineral deposits, no-one has yet suggested that they could be exploited for economic gain.

Why does the Antarctic need protecting?

Antarctica needs protecting because it is a fragile environment where even small amounts of damage can have serious effects on the surroundings and, in particular, wildlife. Some past and present concerns include:

● Pollution around scientific bases in the early days of Antarctic exploration.
● Until recently, overfishing, particularly of krill and whales. See diagram **C** for the effects of overfishing.
● New problems caused by the recent increase of tourism (up to 10,000 visitors a year).

D Satellite image of Antarctica

Weddell Sea

South Pole

Antarctic Circle

Southern Ocean

● International scientific stations

How can the Antarctic be protected?

Since the mid 1980s there has been a growing international awareness of the need to preserve Antarctica. Much progress has been made in recent years. The Protocol on Environmental Protection (1991), for example, aims to make the Antarctic 'a natural reserve devoted to peace and science'.

The Protocol is supported by groups such as Greenpeace and WWF and once it is signed by all 26 active Antarctic nations, will help to protect the entire continent as well as the seas around it. To date, 22 nations have signed the agreement, including the UK. Some ways of protecting the Antarctic are shown in **E**.

E

Some sewage can be released into the sea to provide food for certain birds.

All waste such as empty tins, bottles and plastic must be removed.

New runways for aircraft reduce costs and help scientists reach study sites more easily.

Strict marine pollution controls stop the discharge of fuel from ships.

The Southern Ocean has been made a whale sanctuary. Mining is banned for 50 years.

Fishing has to be sustainable.

Scientists can study global warming, sea level changes and ozone depletion.

Areas of special scientific interest are carefully managed and plants and animals protected.

Visitors are requested not to tread on vegetation and to keep their distance from wildlife.

Krill fishing is now regulated and its importance in the ecosystem is recognised.

Activities

1 Copy out and complete a Fact File on Antarctica using the following table.

Climate	Scenery	Sea resources	Land resources

2 **a)** What is krill?
   b) Why is it important to the Antarctic?
   c) Why is krill being threatened?

3 Draw a star diagram to show at least four reasons why the Antarctic needs protecting.

4 From diagram **E** above:
   a) Give four ways of protecting the sea environment.
   b) Give four ways of protecting the land environment.
   c) Give two ways of supporting scientific research.

Summary

The Antarctic has many very useful resources. It is also one of the few environments not yet spoilt by people. People have to choose which is more important – to use these resources, or to protect the environment.

What are non-renewable and renewable resources?

It is possible to divide the world's natural resources into two groups.

1 **Non-renewable** resources are those which can only be used once. Coal, for example, can only be burnt once. In time these resources will run out.

2 **Renewable** resources can be used over and over again.
   ● Some, like the sun and the wind, will never run out.
   ● Others can only be used again if they are **recycled** (e.g. paper) or if they are not misused by people (e.g. soil).

Energy resources

We all need energy to help us to work and to play. If we work or play hard we give off heat and use up energy. We have to eat and drink to replace this lost energy. Energy in nature also does work and can give off heat. Coal, for example, can be used to work machines and to heat water.

Sketch **A** shows five main types of **non-renewable** energy resources. These have, so far, been easy and quite cheap to use. Coal, oil and natural gas are called **fossil fuels** because they come from the remains (fossils) of plants and animals. As each of these are used to produce energy they all create a lot of pollution (pages 60–61). They are also causing changes in the world's climate.

A

Oil is used for heating, lighting, transport and to produce electricity

Natural gas is used for heating and to produce electricity

Nuclear energy uses a mineral called uranium to produce electricity

Wood is often the only source of energy in countries which do not have a lot of money

Coal is used for heating and to produce electricity

Sketch **B** shows six main types of **renewable** energy resources. These, in comparison with non-renewable types, are more difficult and expensive to use. However, where they can be used they cause far less pollution.

B

Wave energy is produced by wind blowing over the sea

Wind can turn windmills to create energy

Solar energy comes from the sun

Tidal energy can be produced where fast flowing tides enter river estuaries (mouths)

Water, if it is fast flowing and continuous, produces hydro-electricity

Geothermal energy uses heat from inside the earth

E X T R A S

1 What is meant by 'recycling'?

2 List items which you use in a normal day which are, or could be, recycled.

Activities

1 Make a copy of table **C**. Complete it by choosing the correct words from the following list:

- ◆ can only be used once
- ◆ can be used over and over again
- ◆ costs a lot to produce
- ◆ quite cheap to produce
- ◆ causes much pollution
- ◆ causes little pollution

C

Non-renewable	Renewable

2 Complete the following sentences.
   a) Three fossil fuels which give energy are _____, _____ and _____.
   b) Three types of energy using water are _____, _____ and _____.
   c) A hilly place with a wet and windy climate can produce _____ and _____ energy.
   d) A coastal place with a lot of sun and wind can produce _____, _____ and _____ energy.
   e) Uranium gives _____ energy.
   f) Heat from the earth gives _____ energy.

Summary

Natural resources can be divided into non-renewable and renewable resources. Non-renewable resources, which can only be used once, are usually cheaper to use but cause more pollution.

Oil and the environment

Exploitation is a term which you should try to understand. It is when we use or develop something for our own benefit. It means using something selfishly without thinking about how it affects other people or the environment. In this section we will see how our use of oil to make our lives easier and more pleasant can also harm the environment.

The use of any type of energy causes some pollution. The exploitation of fossil fuels, such as oil, can cause much pollution. This means that a lot of careful planning and management is necessary if we are to make the most of fossil fuels while at the same time protecting the environment.

A Stages in the exploitation of oil

1 Exploration for new oil fields either under the ground or the sea

2 Oil is reached by drilling into the ground or under the sea

3 Oil is moved by pipeline or oil tanker to an oil refinery

4 Oil is stored until it is needed

5 At the refinery the oil is turned into petrol for cars or refined for use in power stations

B

C

How can the exploitation of oil harm the environment?

Each stage in the exploitation of oil can threaten the environment in different ways.

On land – large areas have to be cleared when drilling for oil, for laying pipelines and building refineries and terminals (photo **B**). This can:

- destroy natural vegetation and wildlife habitats
- be an eyesore, especially if the area has attractive scenery
- cause noise when drilling for oil and when the refinery is working
- cause fumes to be released into the air when the oil is being refined.

At sea – most of Britain's oil is found under the North Sea or is imported from overseas. It is taken to refineries, which are found in ports, by pipeline or oil tanker.

- Drilling rigs in the North Sea are ugly and can be a hazard to shipping.
- If pipelines break or oil tankers run aground oil can be spilled. This can kill wildlife and pollute beaches (photo **C**).
- If there is an explosion on a drilling rig or oil tanker then serious fires can occur, endangering lives (photo **D**). Smoke causes air pollution (photo **E**).

D

E

F How can oil companies protect the environment?

| 1 | Before drilling begins a study is made of wildlife. |

| 2 | Routes for pipelines and oil tankers are chosen carefully so as to avoid wildlife habitats and attractive scenery. |

| 3 | Once pipelines are laid the ground is restored. |

| 4 | Drilling sites on land are lined with concrete. Sites at sea are surrounded by booms to trap any oil spills. |

| 5 | Refineries are screened behind trees. They can be painted green or dark brown. |

| 6 | Muffles are put on machines to reduce noise. |

| 7 | When the oil is used up, the land is returned to its original use. |

Activities

1 Write out the meaning of *exploitation*.

2 **a)** Show the five stages of oil exploitation by drawing diagram **G** and putting the boxes in the correct order.
  b) Link your boxes by arrows.

3 **a)** Write short newspaper headlines like the ones in **H** to show five more ways by which the exploitation of oil can harm the environment.

G

Storage

Exploration

Refining

Drilling

Transport

b) For two of your headings write short newspaper articles to describe what happened.

H

Oilslick spoils golden sands

Oil refinery noise keeps locals away

E X T R A

Find out at least six different uses of oil.

Summary   The exploitation of any type of energy can damage the environment. Most damage is done by fossil fuels such as oil. However, with careful planning and management the damage can be kept to a minimum.

Electricity and the environment

Most of Britain's electricity is produced in **thermal power stations** (photo **A**). Thermal power is when electricity is produced by heat. Heat is obtained by burning coal and oil. These are two non-renewable fossil fuels (page 56).

Diagram **B** shows a simplified version of what happens in a thermal power station that uses coal. Large amounts of coal are needed to heat water, and turn it into steam. Steam is then used to turn, or drive, a turbine. As the turbine turns, or rotates, it turns another machine called a generator. It is the generator which produces electricity. Later, large amounts of water are used to cool the steam and to condense it back into water. This is done in large cooling towers (photos **A** and **C**).

Can you imagine living without electricity? In what ways does it make our lives easier and more pleasant? Unfortunately, the production of electricity in thermal power stations can seriously harm and pollute our environment. Four types of pollution are labelled ① to ④ on diagram **B**.

A

When coal or oil is burnt to heat water, waste gases are given off. These gases are released into the air from tall chimneys (photo **C**). Two of these gases are very harmful. One is sulphur dioxide, which causes **acid rain** and kills trees and fish. The other is carbon dioxide, which is causing world temperatures to rise. This is called **global warming** (diagram **D**).

1

The buildings, chimneys and cooling towers are unsightly and take up large amounts of land. The pylons that support wires through which electricity is sent to all parts of Britain are also unsightly.

2

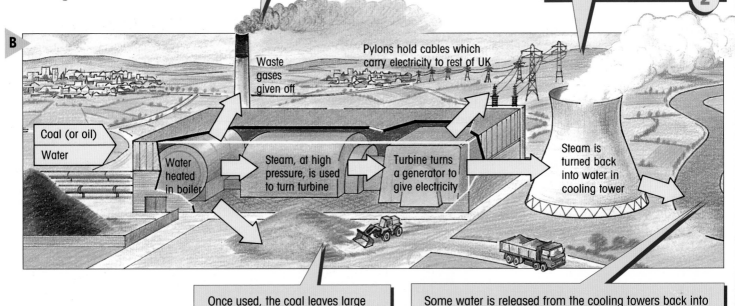

B

Waste gases given off

Pylons hold cables which carry electricity to rest of UK

Coal (or oil)

Water

Water heated in boiler

Steam, at high pressure, is used to turn turbine

Turbine turns a generator to give electricity

Steam is turned back into water in cooling tower

Once used, the coal leaves large amounts of waste ash.

3

Some water is released from the cooling towers back into rivers. As this water is warm, it can kill fish.

4

How can pollution be reduced?

The electricity companies are introducing a way of stopping sulphur dioxide from being released into the air. It is hoped that if limestone is added then it can absorb 90 per cent of the gas. Although this will greatly reduce the effects of acid rain, it will also increase the amount of limestone which has to be quarried. Quarrying often takes place in areas of attractive countryside and can itself spoil the environment (page 21)

Conservation groups favour the use of renewable types of energy to produce electricity (page 57). As yet, these alternative methods are neither as cheap nor as easy to use as fossil fuels. Although wind power may be used by early next century, other forms of power may have to wait until cheaper ways of using them are found or governments become more concerned about protecting the environment.

Several things can be done to reduce the harm done to the environment, but they all cost a lot of money. To pay for these things means putting up the price of electricity. Our problem is that we want cheap electricity and a clean environment. At present we have to choose between them.

C

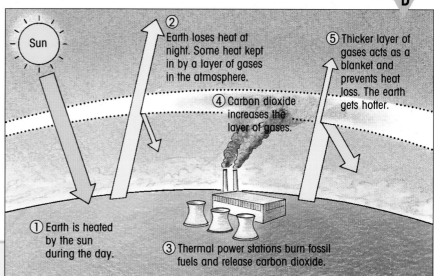

D

① Earth is heated by the sun during the day.

② Earth loses heat at night. Some heat kept in by a layer of gases in the atmosphere.

③ Thermal power stations burn fossil fuels and release carbon dioxide.

④ Carbon dioxide increases the layer of gases.

⑤ Thicker layer of gases acts as a blanket and prevents heat loss. The earth gets hotter.

Sun

Activities

1 a) What is a thermal power station?
   b) Name **two** fossil fuels used in thermal power stations.

2 Photo **A** and diagram **B** show how electricity is produced in a thermal power station. In description **E** the key words have been missed out although their first letters have been given. Copy out the description and fill in the missing words.

3 Describe how the production of electricity can harm the
   a) air
   b) water and
   c) landscape (scenery).

4 Which of the two opinions given in cartoon **F** do you think is more important? Give reasons for your answer.

How e_____ is produced in a thermal power station   E

The power station needs a large area of f_____ land. It needs plenty of c____ to heat w____ to make s____. Waste g____ from the coal are released into the a_____. The steam turns a t____ which turns a g_____ which produces e____. The steam is cooled by water in a c____ t____. Warm water may be released into r____.

It is better to have cheap electricity than to worry about the environment.

The protection of the environment is much more important than cheap electricity.   F

Summary   Using coal and oil are the easiest and cheapest ways to produce electricity, but they also cause the most pollution.

New technology and the oil industry

Many industrialised countries in the world have come to rely on oil. They need it for transport, energy and heating. Oil is a non-renewable resource, and more and more countries use oil. The cheapest sources, and the easiest to use, have been exhausted. Oil is getting more expensive and harder to find and exploit. This means that oil companies have had to improve their **technology**. Technology is when industry finds new ways of doing things and uses new equipment and materials. In the oil industry, improved technology has been needed to find new supplies of oil, then to drill, move and refine that oil.

Map **A** shows where most of the world's oil is found. Oil is often found:
- in areas where the climate and relief make exploration and drilling very difficult (photos **C**, **D** and **E**)
- a long way from the countries that use most of the oil – this makes transport both difficult and expensive (photo **B**).

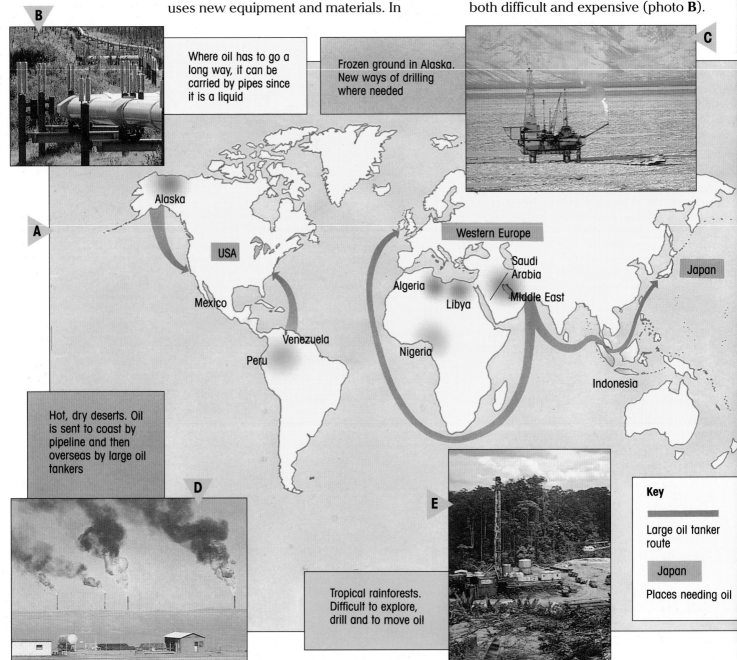

B

Where oil has to go a long way, it can be carried by pipes since it is a liquid

Frozen ground in Alaska. New ways of drilling where needed

C

A

Alaska

USA

Western Europe

Saudi Arabia

Mexico

Algeria

Libya

Middle East

Japan

Venezuela

Nigeria

Peru

Indonesia

Hot, dry deserts. Oil is sent to coast by pipeline and then overseas by large oil tankers

D

E

Tropical rainforests. Difficult to explore, drill and to move oil

Key

▬▬▬ Large oil tanker route

Japan

Places needing oil

The North Sea

Britain uses a lot of oil. At first it came from overseas countries. In the 1960s oil companies began to look for oil under the North Sea. They were able to do this because they developed new technology in underwater **exploration**. When oil was found in 1970 new ways had to be found to **drill** for the oil and then **transport** it to the coast. Improved technology has helped oil companies to drill under the North Sea and to bring oil ashore (diagram **F**).

Once ashore oil cannot be used until it has been refined. Refining gets rid of waste products. It also gives different types of oil which are needed for different purposes.

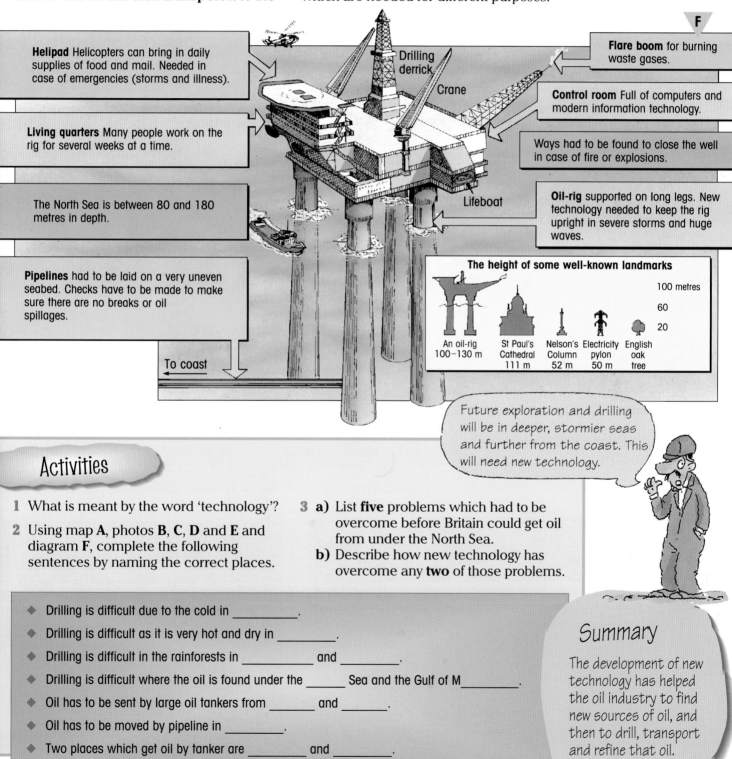

F

Helipad Helicopters can bring in daily supplies of food and mail. Needed in case of emergencies (storms and illness).

Living quarters Many people work on the rig for several weeks at a time.

The North Sea is between 80 and 180 metres in depth.

Pipelines had to be laid on a very uneven seabed. Checks have to be made to make sure there are no breaks or oil spillages.

To coast

Drilling derrick

Crane

Lifeboat

Flare boom for burning waste gases.

Control room Full of computers and modern information technology.

Ways had to be found to close the well in case of fire or explosions.

Oil-rig supported on long legs. New technology needed to keep the rig upright in severe storms and huge waves.

The height of some well-known landmarks

100 metres
60
20

An oil-rig 100–130 m · St Paul's Cathedral 111 m · Nelson's Column 52 m · Electricity pylon 50 m · English oak tree

Future exploration and drilling will be in deeper, stormier seas and further from the coast. This will need new technology.

Activities

1 What is meant by the word 'technology'?

2 Using map **A**, photos **B**, **C**, **D** and **E** and diagram **F**, complete the following sentences by naming the correct places.

3 **a)** List **five** problems which had to be overcome before Britain could get oil from under the North Sea.
   b) Describe how new technology has overcome any **two** of those problems.

◆ Drilling is difficult due to the cold in _____.

◆ Drilling is difficult as it is very hot and dry in _____.

◆ Drilling is difficult in the rainforests in _____ and _____.

◆ Drilling is difficult where the oil is found under the _____ Sea and the Gulf of M_____.

◆ Oil has to be sent by large oil tankers from _____ and _____.

◆ Oil has to be moved by pipeline in _____.

◆ Two places which get oil by tanker are _____ and _____.

Summary

The development of new technology has helped the oil industry to find new sources of oil, and then to drill, transport and refine that oil.

5 Population

Are we evenly spread?

There are about 57 million people in the United Kingdom but where do they all live? Map **A** shows this. It is a **population distribution** map and shows how people are spread out across the country. You can easily see that the population is not evenly spread out. There are some areas with a lot of people and some with very few. The south and east seem to be most crowded, and the north and west the least crowded.

The map uses **density** to show how crowded places are. Density is the number of people in an area. It is worked out by dividing the total population by the total area and is usually given as the number of people per square kilometre. Places that are crowded are said to be **densely populated** and to have a high population density. Places with few people are said to be **sparsely populated** and to have a low population density.

The most crowded places of all are towns and cities. In Britain today almost 9 out of 10 people live in a town or city. Some towns and cities are shown on map **A** and in table **C**. London is by far the largest and most densely populated city in the United Kingdom. Almost 7 million people live there, and in the most crowded inner city areas there are up to 10,000 people in a square kilometre.

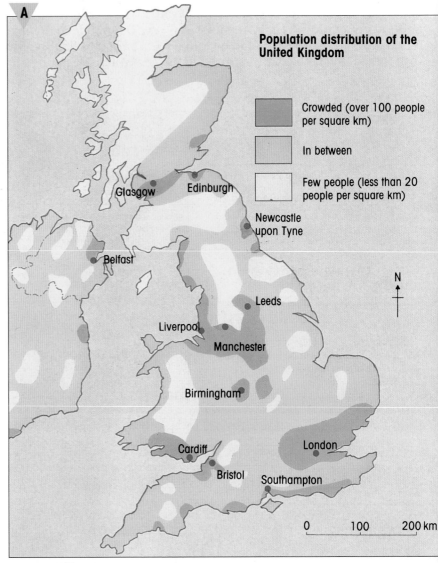

A

Population distribution of the United Kingdom

Crowded (over 100 people per square km)

In between

Few people (less than 20 people per square km)

Glasgow Edinburgh
Newcastle upon Tyne
Belfast
Leeds
Liverpool
Manchester
Birmingham
Cardiff London
Bristol Southampton

N

0   100   200 km

B

It's very beautiful and quiet here but there's not a lot to do.

Why do we all crowd together? Why don't we spread out a bit?

It's nice to be with other people and have shops, jobs, entertainments and other things nearby.

C

Population of some cities in Britain
(figures are in thousands)

Belfast	297	Leeds	724
Birmingham	1,008	Liverpool	474
Bristol	399	London	6,967
Cardiff	414	Manchester	431
Edinburgh	444	Newcastle	284
Glasgow	680	Southampton	212

Note: Some of these cities are part of larger urban areas with populations greater than those given in the table. Figures are for 1994 (estimated).

Photos **D** and **E** show places with very different population densities. Photo **D** is a typical city scene with many buildings, plenty of activity and a lot of people. Photo **E** was taken in Scotland. It shows part of the Highlands, a beautiful but sparsely populated area in the north.

Can you think why one place is crowded whilst the other has very few people? What is the area like where you live – is it crowded or is it sparsely populated? Can you suggest why it has that population density?

D

E

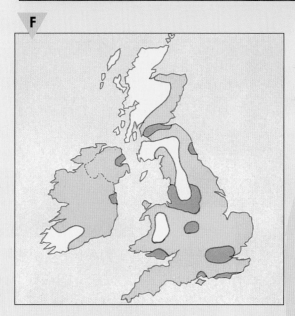

Activities

1 Copy and complete these sentences.
   a) A **population distribution** map shows . . .
   b) **Population density** tells us . . .
   c) **Densely populated** means that . . .
   d) **Sparsely populated** means that . . .

2 Map **F** shows the spread of population in Britain.
   a) Make a copy of the map and complete the key.
   b) Write a paragraph to describe the distribution of population. Include the following words in your description:
   spread • unevenly • south and east • densely • north and west • sparsely

3 **a)** List the cities from table **C** in order of size. Give the biggest first.
   b) Give three advantages of living in cities.

4 Look at sketch **B** and think carefully about what people need to live their everyday lives.
   a) Study photo **D** and make a list of the things that would help people to live there.
   b) Study photo **E** and suggest why very few people live in that area.

F

EXTRA

Draw a bar graph to show the number of people in each of the cities in table **C**.
- Arrange the bars in order of size with the biggest on the left.
- Use different colours for the cities in England, Scotland, Wales and Northern Ireland.
- Give your graph a title.

Summary

People are not spread evenly over Britain. Some areas are very crowded whilst others are almost empty. Population density is a measure of how crowded an area is.

Now where's the best place to live?

What affects where we live?

Not only is the distribution of population uneven in Britain, but it is uneven throughout the world. There are now over 5,000 million people in the world yet most of them live on only a third of the land surface. Like Britain, some areas are very crowded and others are almost empty.

There are many reasons for this. People do not like to live in places which are too wet or too dry, too hot or too cold. Nor do they like places that are mountainous, lack vegetation, are densely forested or liable to flood. People prefer pleasant places in which to live. They want to be able to earn money by working and have food available through farming or from shops. They like to be near to other people and have things to do and places to go.

Factors that discourage people from settling in an area are called **negative factors**. Factors that encourage people to live in an area are called **positive factors**. Some of these are shown in the photos below and in diagram **G** on the next page.

Look carefully at the photos and for each one in turn try to work out why it is likely to be either a densely populated area or a sparsely populated area.

A Himalayan Mountains

B Amazon Forest

C Western Europe

D Sahara Desert

E Polar regions – Antarctica

F Bangladesh

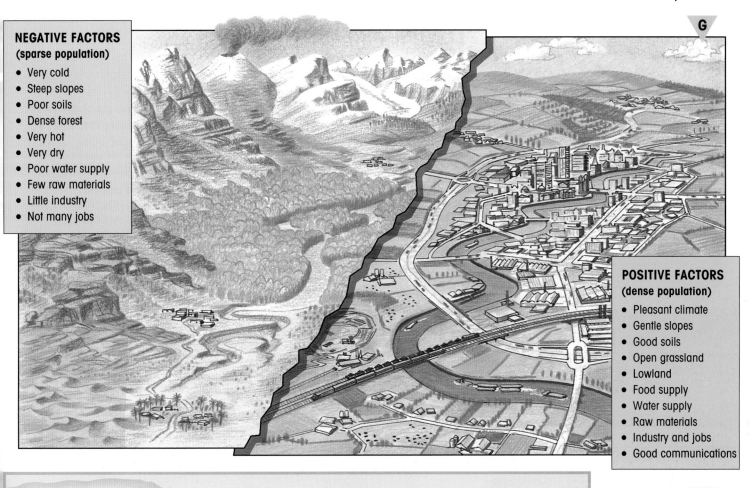

NEGATIVE FACTORS
(sparse population)

- Very cold
- Steep slopes
- Poor soils
- Dense forest
- Very hot
- Very dry
- Poor water supply
- Few raw materials
- Little industry
- Not many jobs

POSITIVE FACTORS
(dense population)

- Pleasant climate
- Gentle slopes
- Good soils
- Open grassland
- Lowland
- Food supply
- Water supply
- Raw materials
- Industry and jobs
- Good communications

G

Activities

1 a) Which one of the photos **A** to **F** does this list of words and phrases best describe:
steep slopes • snowy • icy • very cold • mountainous • no soil • no industry • very few people?

b) Which of these could be used to describe photo **F**:
hot • cold • wet • dry • steep • level • poor soils • good farming • factory work • many people • sparse population?

c) Imagine that you are passing through the desert in photo **D**. Make a list of words and phrases to describe what it would be like. Try to give at least **eight** different things.

2 Draw table **H** and put the following into the correct columns:

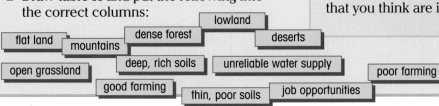

flat land · mountains · lowland · dense forest · deserts · open grassland · deep, rich soils · unreliable water supply · poor farming · good farming · thin, poor soils · job opportunities

Sparsely populated (negative factors)	Densely populated (positive factors)

H

3 Give **two** reasons why few people live in
a) mountain areas
b) desert areas.

E X T R A

Is the place where you live crowded or sparsely populated? What are the reasons for this? List the factors from diagram **G** which affect your area. Add any others that you think are important.

Summary

The way people are spread across the world is affected by many different things. These include relief, climate, vegetation, water supply, raw materials and employment opportunities.

Where do we live?

The photo-map below is quite remarkable. It is made up from more than 37 million satellite images carefully put together to give a picture of the world. The red dots have been added to show the distribution of population. Look carefully and you can see many of the world's major features. The cold **polar regions** show up as white. The densely forested parts of South America and Africa are a lush green. The areas that are dry and lacking vegetation are shades of brown. Can you see the great mountain ranges? They show up as patches or streaks of white.

The map also confirms how unevenly people are spread over the world. Vast areas have hardly any people living in them whilst other areas seem to be very crowded. Try to name some of the emptiest places. Places with a lot of people include parts of Western Europe, India, China and Japan. Where else in the world does the photo-map show that there are a lot of people?

Photos of the six areas described below are shown on page 66.

A

Amazon Forest
Too hot and wet for people.
Dense forest makes communications and settlement difficult.
Sparsely populated.

Western Europe
Low-lying and gently sloping.
Pleasant climate.
Good water supply and soil for farming.
Easy communications and many resources for industry.
Densely populated.

Himalayan Mountains
Too cold for people.
Steep slopes are bad for communications and settlement.
Poor, thin soil unsuitable for crops.
Sparsely populated.

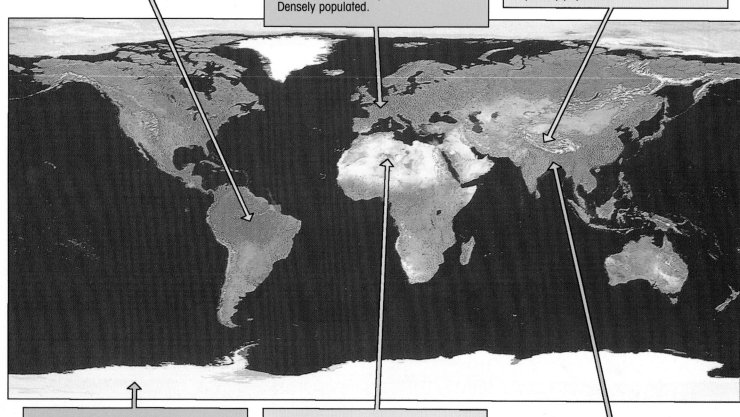

Polar regions – Antarctica
Too cold for people.
No soil for crops.
Snow and ice make communications and settlement very difficult.
Sparsely populated.

Sahara Desert
Too hot and dry for people.
Too dry and too little soil for crops to grow.
Sand makes communications difficult.
Sparsely populated.

Bangladesh
Low-lying and flat.
Rich, fertile soil. Hot and wet.
Ideal farming conditions.
Densely populated.

Cities are very popular places in which to live. They can provide housing, jobs, education, medical care and a better chance of getting on and enjoying life. More than half the world's population now live in cities and the number is increasing all the time.

The fastest growing cities tend to be in the poorer countries. Here, the urban population is expected to double in the next ten years. This will produce some very large cities.

One of these, Mexico City, is expected to overtake Tokyo, and become the largest city in the world by the year 2000. By then it will have a population of more than 31 million. At present its size is increasing by over half a million people a year. That is the same as all the inhabitants of Liverpool or Edinburgh suddenly arriving in Mexico City in a single year. Think of the problems that such a rapid increase must cause.

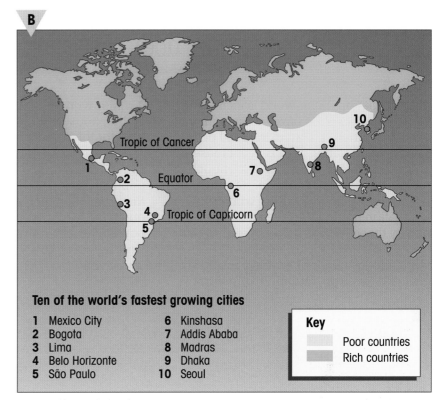

Ten of the world's fastest growing cities

1	Mexico City	6	Kinshasa
2	Bogota	7	Addis Ababa
3	Lima	8	Madras
4	Belo Horizonte	9	Dhaka
5	São Paulo	10	Seoul

Key
- Poor countries
- Rich countries

Activities

1 Copy and complete the sentences below using the following words:

densely · uneven · sparsely · deserts · polar regions

a) The distribution of population over the world is _____.

b) The areas with the fewest people are the dense forests, _____ and _____.

c) Mountainous areas are _____ populated.

d) Areas with good resources and industry are _____ populated.

2 Give named examples of:
a) four densely populated areas
b) six sparsely populated areas.

3 Which of the fastest growing cities are in:
a) South America
b) Africa
c) Asia?

4 Of the eight statements given below, three are correct. Write out the correct ones.
The ten fastest growing cities are
- in poor countries.
- in rich countries.
- mainly in polar regions.
- mainly between the tropics.
- on the coast.
- spread all over the world.
- in one continent.
- in South America, Africa and Asia.

5 Copy star diagram **C** and complete your diagram to show six reasons why people like to live in cities.

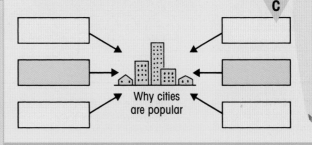

Why cities are popular

E X T R A S

1 Use an atlas to name a country for each of the fastest growing cities in map **B**.

2 With help from an atlas, try to find out why central Australia is sparsely populated and east and south-west USA are densely populated.

Summary

People are not spread evenly over the world. Some of the most crowded places are in China, India, parts of Western Europe, and some areas of Africa and the USA. More and more people in the world are living in cities.

How does population change?

The population of the world is increasing very quickly. Experts have worked out that every hour there are an extra 8,000 people living on our planet. That is an increase of about 2 people every second or enough people to fill a city the size of Birmingham in about a week. In 1987 the world's population passed the 5,000 million mark and by the year 2000 it is expected to be over 6,000 million. This increase in population is now so fast that it is often described as a **population explosion**.

A major world problem is how to feed, clothe, house, educate, provide jobs and care for this rapidly increasing population.

Graph **A** shows the changes in world population since the year 1100. Notice how the population increase is not even. Until one hundred or two hundred years ago the population growth was actually very slow. Only in recent times has there been a real 'explosion'.

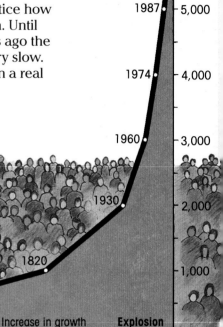

A

Millions of people
- 6,000
- 1987 — 5,000
- 1974 — 4,000
- 1960 — 3,000
- 1930
- 2,000
- 1820
- 1,000
- 1650
- 0

Population in AD 1 estimated to have been 250 million

Slow growth · Increase in growth · **Explosion**

Year 1100 1200 1300 1400 1500 1600 1700 1800 1900 2000

Population increases when the number of babies being born is greater than the number of people dying. The number of babies being born each year is called the **birth rate**. The number of people who die each year is called the **death rate**. Birth rates and death rates are measured as the number of births and deaths for each 1,000 of the population. The speed at which the population increases is called the **population growth rate**. Diagrams **B**, **C** and **D** show how the balance between births and deaths affects the population growth.

B

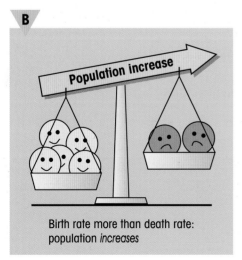

Birth rate more than death rate: population *increases*

C

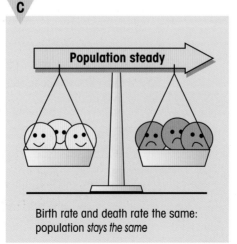

Birth rate and death rate the same: population *stays the same*

D

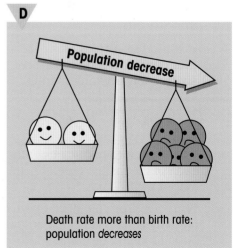

Death rate more than birth rate: population *decreases*

The population growth rate is not the same for all countries. In some, like Britain, the difference between birth and death rates is small so the population is changing only very slowly. In other countries, like Bangladesh, there are big differences between birth and death rates so the population is increasing rapidly.

E

Country	Birth rate	Death rate	Natural increase
Bangladesh	41	14	27
Brazil	26	8	18
China	21	7	14
France	13	10	3
India	31	10	21
Italy	11	10	1
Japan	12	8	4
Mexico	27	5	22
UK	14	12	2
USA	14	9	5

(1994)

- Figures given per 1,000 people.
- Poorer countries are shaded yellow.
- **Natural increase** is the difference between birth and death rates.

Table **E** shows birth and death rates for some countries. Remember, the greater the difference between births and deaths, the larger the population change will be.

F   Things that can affect birth and death rates

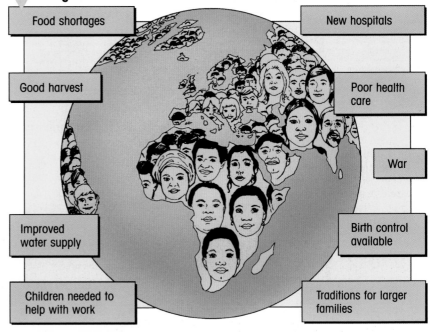

Food shortages

New hospitals

Good harvest

Poor health care

War

Improved water supply

Birth control available

Children needed to help with work

Traditions for larger families

Activities

1 **a)** When did the world's population reach 1,000 million?
   b) How long did it take to double to 2,000 million?
   c) How long did it take to double again to 4,000 million?

E X T R A S

1 Draw table **H** below and from diagram **F** sort the things that affect birth rates and death rates into the correct columns.

H

Birth rate		Death rate	
High	Low	High	Low

2 Suggest **three** reasons why people in the UK may be more likely to live longer than people in poorer countries.

2 Describe the increase in world population shown in graph **A**.

3 **a)** Write a sentence to explain what each of the following terms means.
   - Birth rate
   - Death rate
   - Population growth rate
   b) Why is 'explosion' a good description of population changes since 1950?

4 Copy and complete table **G** below by writing **increase**, **same** or **decrease** in the last column.

G

Births	Deaths	Population change
→	→	
→	→	
→	→	
→	→	

5 **a)** List the countries from table **E** by the size of their natural increase. Put the one with the greatest increase first.
   b) What do you notice about the richer and the poorer countries?

Summary

The world's population is increasing at a very rapid rate. Growth is very much faster in the poorer countries than in the richer ones. Population changes in a country depend mainly on the birth and death rates.

What is migration?

Mexico City is one of the largest cities in the world. It is also one of the fastest growing. This is partly because of natural increase but mainly because like most cities, it acts like a magnet and attracts people from other places to live there.

People who move from one place to another to live or work are called **migrants**. They have a big effect on populations because they increase the numbers and can alter the 'mix' of people who are living in a place.

Graph **A** shows how quickly Mexico City has grown since 1940. The photos in **C** show some people who have migrated to Mexico City. Notice how different they look and what varied backgrounds they have. Their comments may help to explain some of the reasons why people migrate.

A **Population of Mexico City**

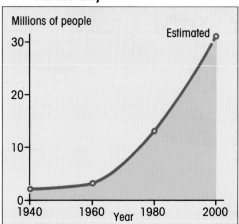

B Mexico City

C

Pedro

I'm from a village down on the coast and was injured in an accident. My family live in Mexico City so I've come to join them. I hope to get good medical care here.

Maria

I went to college in Acapulco but I'm ambitious and think that I'll have a better chance of getting a good job and enjoying life in Mexico's capital city.

Janine

I've just qualified as a nurse in New York. I came to Mexico City so that I could help people who are less well off than myself.

Carlos

I came here from Spain. My company in Madrid sent me to Mexico City some years ago and I like it so much that I'm going to stay.

Zina

I've lived here all my life but I'm descended from slaves who were brought across from Africa many years ago.

Taxa

I was brought up in a small Indian village in the mountains. I had very little future there because conditions were primitive and there were no proper jobs or education.

Migration is when people move home. The movement may be just around the corner to a better house. It may be from one part of the country to another in search of a job. It might be from one country to another for a different way of life. For many people country areas have very little to offer so they move to the towns and cities. This is called **rural-to-urban migration**. For other people a move to a different country holds many attractions. This is called **international migration**.

People migrate for two reasons. Firstly, they may wish to get away from things that they do not like. These are called **push factors** and include a shortage of jobs and poor living conditions. Secondly, people are attracted to things that they do like. These are called **pull factors** and include pleasant surroundings and good medical care.

D

PUSH FACTORS

- Political fears
- Not enough jobs
- Few opportunities
- Natural disasters
- Wars
- Unhappy life
- Shortage of food

PULL FACTORS

Hope for
- Better way of life
- Chances of a job
- Improved living conditions
- Education
- Better housing
- Medical care
- Family links

Activities

1 What do each of these terms mean?
  - Migration
  - Rural-to-urban migration
  - International migration

2 a) Copy and complete bar graph **E** to show population growth in Mexico City.
  b) Describe the increase in Mexico City's population since 1940. Use your graph and graph **A** to help you. Give actual figures.
  c) Suggest reasons for this growth.

E

Year	Millions of people
2000	31 million (estimated)
1980	13 million
1960	3 million

0   10   20   30
Millions of people

3 a) What is a push factor? Give two examples.
  b) What is a pull factor? Give two examples.

4 Copy table **F** and use it to explain why the people in **C** migrated to Mexico City.

F

	Push factor	Pull factor
Pedro		
Janine		
Zina		
Maria		
Carlos		
Taxa		

5 Imagine you are a migrant like Taxa in **C**.
  a) You have just arrived in Mexico City. Describe your first few days there. Think about getting a job, food, shelter, making friends . . .
  b) You left your village because of poor conditions there. What attracted you to the city?

Summary

Migration is the movement of people from one place to another. This movement may be the result of push and pull factors. The migration of people affects population size and the variety of different people in a place.

Why migrate to America?

The United States has much to offer migrants. It is a place with many opportunities, high standards of living, and an attractive way of life. It is one of the wealthiest places in the world, jobs are readily available, education is good and health care is excellent. All these things put together are sometimes called the 'American Dream' – a vision of freedom, opportunity and good living which is available for all.

For people living in the world's poorer countries, the USA is very attractive. Since 1940 many Mexicans have migrated northwards into the USA. They seek the 'American Dream' but most of all they go in search of work and the chance to earn money. They hope to rid themselves of the poverty and unemployment of Mexico and replace that with what they hope will be the wealth and opportunity of the USA.

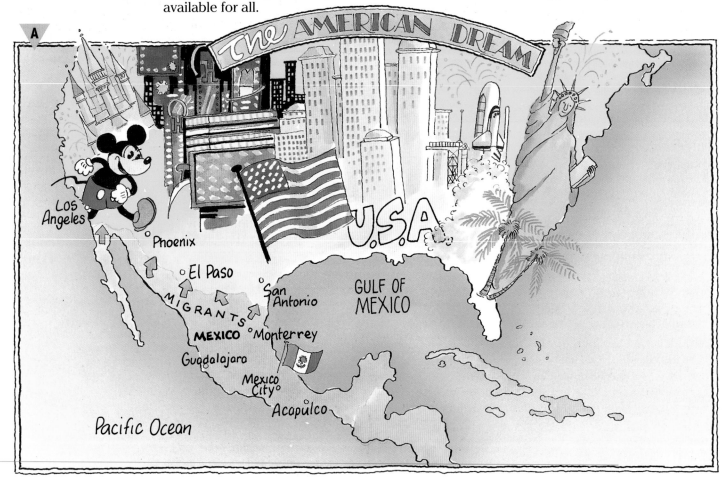

Most Mexicans settle in California or Texas. Some cross the border legally but perhaps as many as two million a year cross without permission. Many Mexicans now live permanently in the USA but some stay there only on a temporary basis. Some **temporary migrants** take jobs that are **seasonal** and when the work is finished they return to Mexico. Others cross the border every day to work then return home at night. These people are called **migrant workers**.

Migrant workers do all kinds of work. Many work on large farms and in food processing factories (page 27). Others work in the cities where they often gain employment on construction projects, and in hotels and restaurants. Most do unskilled and low paid work but even in those occupations they can earn more in a month than they could in a full year in Mexico.

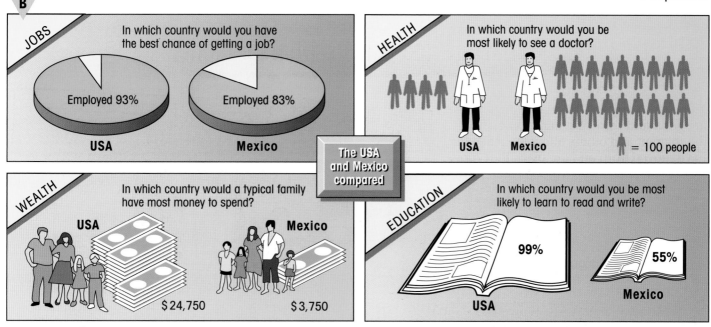

B

JOBS — In which country would you have the best chance of getting a job?

Employed 93% — **USA**
Employed 83% — **Mexico**

The USA and Mexico compared

HEALTH — In which country would you be most likely to see a doctor?

USA   Mexico   👤 = 100 people

WEALTH — In which country would a typical family have most money to spend?

USA — $ 24,750
Mexico — $ 3,750

EDUCATION — In which country would you be most likely to learn to read and write?

99% — **USA**
55% — **Mexico**

Activities

1 Copy diagram **C** and complete it to show **six** things that make up the 'American Dream'.

C

The American Dream

2 **a)** Copy and complete table **D** below using information from diagram **B**.
  b) Explain why Mexicans are keen to migrate to the USA.

D

	USA	Mexico
Unemployment		
People per doctor		
Family income		
School attendance		

3 Diagram **E** shows how much a sewing machinist earns each week in the garment making trade.
  a) Why do Mexicans like working in the USA?
  b) Why do Americans like to employ Mexicans?
  c) How does Mexican migrant labour help America to be prosperous?

E

Mexico **$15**   Migrant in USA **$150**   US average **$ 300**

4 On the right is a list of jobs that Mexican migrants do. Sort the jobs under the headings:

waitress • cook • nurse • fruit picker • electrician • farm labourer • rubbish collector • sewing machinist • petrol station attendant • construction worker

Low paid	Seasonal	Skilful

E X T R A S

1 Imagine that you are to migrate to America. What would you like most about the place if you were
  a) a 12-year-old child
  b) a parent with three children?

2 Draw a poster showing the advantages of living in the USA rather than in Mexico.

Summary

Migrants usually move from poor places to the nearest rich place. Many Mexicans migrate to their nearest neighbour, the USA. They move in the hope of gaining employment and a better chance in life.

What are the effects of migration?

There are many effects of migration. Some are good and some are bad. Some affect the migrant and others affect the place they have moved from and the place they move to. Look at sketches **B** and **C**, which show some of these effects.

A

B Migration – the good...and the bad

> It's great here...we love it! Jose got a job straight away in a clothing factory. We have a small flat and the children are at a local school. We are all making progress with the language and have already made lots of friends. Migration was a good move for us...we are really very happy.

The Sanchez family

> I wish we had never left Mexico. We can't speak the language and have had great difficulty getting work and making friends. It's been hard finding a reasonable place to live because we have so little money and people just don't seem to want to help us. Migration has made us homesick and very unhappy.

The Pancho family

> I think the Mexicans are great. I can't afford to pay high wages but the Mexicans seem to be happy on low pay so that's good for my business and I'm happy to employ them. I think we should encourage Mexicans to live in America because they do jobs that we don't like and they are good for our economy

Eddie Ingle, restaurant owner

> I'm sick of these Mexicans coming into our country. They take our jobs, live in our houses and try to change our cities to suit their way of life. I don't have a job and I really don't think it's fair that a foreigner should get work before me.

Brad Bradley, unemployed

Activities

1 **a)** Give **five** reasons why the Sanchez family are pleased they migrated to America.
   b) Give **five** reasons why the Pancho family are unhappy after migrating to America.

2 In the spiral **D** there are five effects of migration. Find them by starting at the centre and working outwards. Sort the effects into **Good** and **Bad**.

3 Write out the following statements that are **true**.
   Migrant workers
   - stop local people getting jobs.
   - all live in California.
   - help keep factories open.
   - have large families.
   - work long hours.
   - change the way of life.

4 Suggest reasons for the headlines in **E**. Answer in the form of a short newspaper article for each one.

D

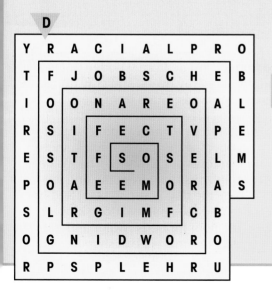

California Herald
LOCAL BUSINESSES WELCOME MIGRANTS

Los Angeles Star
California to restrict entry of migrants

E

TEXAS TIMES
Unions complain about migrant workers

EXTRA

Work with a partner. One of you be Eddie Ingle and the other Brad Bradley.
- Make two lists, one to show the good things about migrants and the other the bad things. Rank the items in each list in order of importance.
- Display your lists on a large sheet of paper. Add a title and drawings to make it more effective.

Summary

Many Mexicans settle happily in their new surroundings but for some there can be difficulties. Migrants can be a great help to the American economy. They often provide cheap labour and work at jobs which local people are reluctant to do.

Kenya — what is the Maasai way of life?

Jambo! A developing country is usually quite poor like Kenya in Africa.

'Jambo' (hello) is the greeting always given by Kenyans. Kenya is an **economically developing country** located on the Equator in East Africa. By 'developing', we mean that it has less **capital** (money) and fewer services compared with a **developed** country like the UK. The landscape of Kenya is varied and beautiful and although there are many different **ethnic** groups living in the country, there is little tension between them. 'Ethnic' means a group of people who have a similar language, religion and way of life. Each ethnic group in Kenya has a different pattern of daily life.

The Maasai in Kenya

One ethnic group living in Kenya are the Maasai (see map **A** on page 82). They are **pastoralists** with herds of cattle and goats. Some are **nomadic** and have to move about to find water and grass for their animals. The Maasai depend on these animals for their daily food. It is cattle, not money, which means wealth to the Maasai. Indeed, the usual Maasai greeting is 'I hope your cows are well'. The land where the Maasai live is fairly flat and covered with grass which depends upon the rain. The 'long rains' come between April and June, the 'short rains' in October and November. In the dry months the grass withers under the hot sun. If the rains do not come then the Maasai have to move to look for grass for their animals.

A

B

Houses

Most Maasai live in an **enkang** which is a small village made up of 20 to 50 huts (photo **A**), in which 10 to 20 families live. It is surrounded by a thick thorn hedge to keep out dangerous animals such as lions, leopards and hyenas. Tiny passages allow people and, in the evening, cattle to pass through. These passages are blocked up at night. The huts are built in a circle around an open central area. They barely reach the height of an adult Maasai (photo **B** and plan **C**) and are built from local materials.

The frame is made from wooden poles. Mud, from nearby rivers, and cow dung are used for the walls. Grass from the surrounding area is used for the roof. The hut is entered by a narrow tunnel. Apart from an opening the size of a brick, there are no windows or chimneys. The inside is dark and full of smoke from the fire. It is cool during the day, warm at night and free from flies and mosquitoes. Cowskins are laid on the floor for beds. Water and honey are stored in gourds – a ball shaped plant with a thick skin.

C

Plan of the inside of a Maasai hut

← 4 metres →

Bed – hides on the floor

Warm area for newly born cattle

Store for water and food

4 metres

Wood store

Open fire

Bed – hides on the floor

Small tunnel as entrance

D

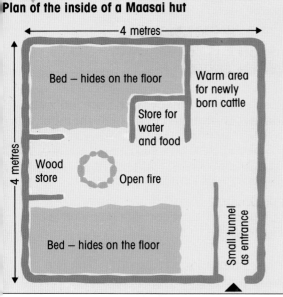

Dress

Men wear brightly coloured 'blankets' and women wear lengths of cloth (photo **A**). The women shave their heads and wear beads around their neck, wrists and ankles. Teeth are cleaned with sticks and the men also use sticks to comb their hair. As water is often scarce, the Maasai use animal and vegetable fat to clean themselves and sweet smelling grasses for perfume.

Daily jobs

The women have to collect sticks for the fire, and water for cooking. They also make baskets and jewellery. The men spend the whole day guarding their animals. The Maasai regard the ground as sacred and believe it should not be broken. This means no crops can be grown, wells cannot be dug and, often, the dead are not buried but are left to wild animals. As crops are not grown sometimes animals are exchanged for grain.

Diet

A major part of the Maasai diet is milk mixed with blood from their cows. In times of drought only blood is used.

E

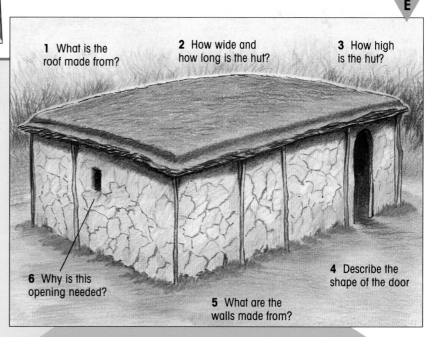

1 What is the roof made from?

2 How wide and how long is the hut?

3 How high is the hut?

4 Describe the shape of the door

5 What are the walls made from?

6 Why is this opening needed?

Activities

1 **a)** Give two facts about a developing country.
   b) What is meant by 'an ethnic group'?
   c) In which continent is Kenya?

2 **a)** Give two reasons why cattle are important to the Maasai.
   b) Write a paragraph to describe Maasai farming. Include these words: *cattle and goats, flat land, grass, rain, nomadic*.

3 Sketch **E** shows a Maasai hut and several questions. Draw the hut and add labels by answering the questions.

4 How do photo **A** and your drawing of a Maasai hut suggest that the weather is:
   a) usually warm
   b) not very wet?

Summary

Landscape, weather and wealth all affect the family life, housing, clothing and diet of the Maasai.

The Kikuyu and their environment

The largest ethnic group living in Kenya are the **Kikuyu**. Their home region is in the higher parts of the country between Mount Kenya and the capital city of Nairobi (see map **A** on page 82). Of all the ethnic groups it is the Kikuyu who have adapted most easily to western culture.

Settlement

Traditionally the Kikuyu lived in small, circular and fairly **nucleated** villages. These were similar to those of the Maasai with whom they had friendly contact. Today, driving through this part of Kenya, a visitor will see two types of settlement which have replaced these villages.

Most houses are **dispersed**. Each individual house is surrounded by a small **shamba** or garden (photo **A**). The family try to grow their yearly supply of food in the shamba. The house is circular and built from local materials. The walls are made from wooden poles tied together and the thatched roof from coconut palm leaves and grass.

Houses next to roads are often built in a **linear** pattern forming villages and small towns. Planks of wood are used for the walls and corrugated iron for the roof. The insides become very warm during the day and cold at night.

A

B

Land use and jobs

Most of the land is used for farming. The Kikuyu, unlike the Maasai, grow crops and keep very few animals. Farming is easier here because there is more rain and it is more reliable. The natural forest adds **humus** to the already deep soils. There are two types of farming in this area – **subsistence** and **commercial**.

Subsistence farming means a family grows just enough food for themselves and has very little left over to sell (photo **B**). Most shambas grow maize under the shade of small banana trees (photo **A**). Beans, yams and millet are grown as well as many tropical fruits and vegetables. No land is wasted.

Commercial farming means that crops are grown on a large scale. Earlier this century the Kikuyu lands were turned into plantations by British farmers. **Plantations** are large estates, usually found in the tropics, where the natural forest is cleared and one main crop is planted in rows. In this part of Kenya the main crop is coffee on the lower slopes and tea on the higher slopes (photo **C**). Both crops need a lot of back-breaking labour and once picked are sold overseas. Today the large plantations have been broken up into smaller units and are farmed by the Kikuyu. Although they provide income for Kenya, these crops do not feed the local people.

C

D

Where the slopes become too steep for farming and settlement the land is left as forest. This protects the ground from soil erosion and provides the people with firewood for cooking and warmth. In Kenya, as in many developing countries, the women have the hard job of collecting firewood (photo **D**).

The Kikuyu are well known for their crafts which they make both for themselves and

E

to sell in the market and in larger towns (photo **E**). The women make baskets, jewellery and clothes, and the men produce the ironwork.

Activities

1 Sketch **F** shows a Kikuyu house with its shamba or garden, and several questions. Draw the house and add labels by answering the questions.

2 Give **three** reasons why the Kikuyu find farming easier than the Maasai. Think about water supply and soils.

3 **a)** What is a plantation?
   b) Draw a star diagram to describe plantation farming in Kenya. Your diagram should try to answer the following questions:
   ● What happens to the forest?
   ● Which two crops are planted?
   ● On which type of slope is each crop planted?
   ● Where are the crops sold?
   c) Give one **advantage** and one **disadvantage** of plantation farming.

4 Apart from farming, what other jobs are done by Kikuyu men and women?

F

2 How high is the hut?
3 What is the shape of the roof?
1 Name the main tree crop
4 What is the shape of the hut?
5 What is the hut made from?
7 Name the main crop
6 What is the garden around the hut called?

Summary

The settlement, land use and jobs of a locality in a developing country are usually related to the environment.

Why is Kenya's population unevenly spread?

Some of the oldest known human bones have been found in Kenya.

The population of Kenya, as in most other countries, is not spread out evenly. Some places are very crowded while others have very few people living there. This is mainly due to:

● **migration** – where the people of Kenya originally came from
● **physical conditions** – differences in climate and relief in Kenya.

The movement of people into Kenya

Most present-day Kenyans are descended from African tribes who arrived in the country from three main directions (map **A**).

● Those from the north-east are fewest in number and live in the most sparsely populated area (area **W**).
● Those from the south-west are largest in number and live in the most densely populated areas (areas **X**).
● Those from the north-west live in areas which have an average population density for Kenya (area **Y**).
● Map **A** also shows that some Arabs and Indians have migrated to Kenya from the east (area **Z**). These account for only 2 per cent of the total population.

While individual tribes still remain today, their way of life has been changed through marriages with people from other ethnic groups.

Differences in physical conditions

Although Kenya is not a very large country, the physical conditions vary considerably from place to place. Map **B** shows how the distribution of population is affected by differences in rainfall, temperature, water supply, relief, soil and vegetation.

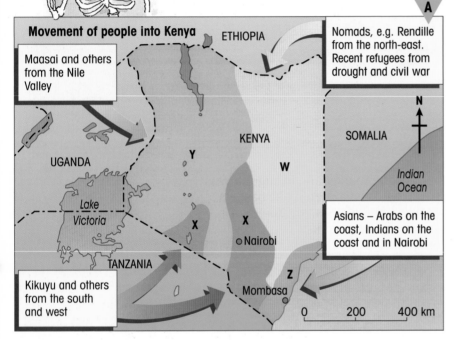

A

Movement of people into Kenya

Maasai and others from the Nile Valley

Nomads, e.g. Rendille from the north-east. Recent refugees from drought and civil war

Asians – Arabs on the coast, Indians on the coast and in Nairobi

Kikuyu and others from the south and west

ETHIOPIA
KENYA
SOMALIA
Indian Ocean
UGANDA
Lake Victoria
TANZANIA
○ Nairobi
Mombasa
0   200   400 km
N

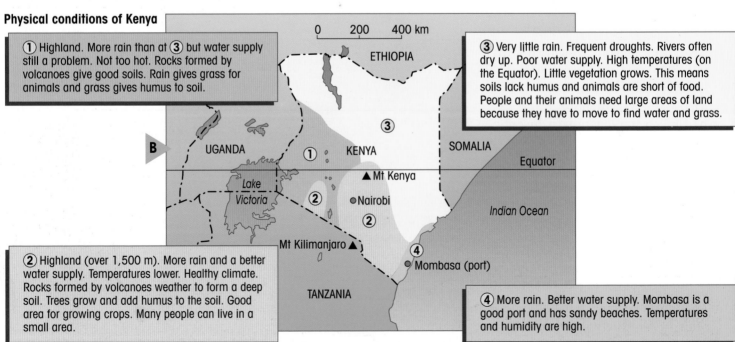

Physical conditions of Kenya

B

① Highland. More rain than at ③ but water supply still a problem. Not too hot. Rocks formed by volcanoes give good soils. Rain gives grass for animals and grass gives humus to soil.

③ Very little rain. Frequent droughts. Rivers often dry up. Poor water supply. High temperatures (on the Equator). Little vegetation grows. This means soils lack humus and animals are short of food. People and their animals need large areas of land because they have to move to find water and grass.

② Highland (over 1,500 m). More rain and a better water supply. Temperatures lower. Healthy climate. Rocks formed by volcanoes weather to form a deep soil. Trees grow and add humus to the soil. Good area for growing crops. Many people can live in a small area.

④ More rain. Better water supply. Mombasa is a good port and has sandy beaches. Temperatures and humidity are high.

0   200   400 km
ETHIOPIA
UGANDA
KENYA
SOMALIA
Equator
▲ Mt Kenya
Lake Victoria
○ Nairobi
Indian Ocean
Mt Kilimanjaro ▲
Mombasa (port)
TANZANIA

Present-day movements of population

In all developing countries there is a large movement of people from the countryside to the towns (see rural-to-urban migration, page 73). In Kenya it is mainly the Kikuyu who move. Their traditional home is in area ② on map **B**.

When driving through rural Kikuyu countryside it is hard to see why they want to move (photo **A**, page 80). It is one of the few parts of Kenya with roads, it has the best farmland and water supply in the country and the environment appears clean and pleasant. To those living there, especially those at school or just starting a family, it is less attractive.

Diagram **C** gives some of the reasons why many Kikuyu want to move to Nairobi, the capital of Kenya.

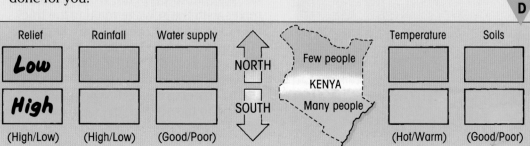

C

> Nairobi has big, modern buildings which include hospitals, shops, cinemas and a university.

> Kenya has one of the highest birth rates in the world. The average family size is 7.6 people. There are too many of us to find jobs on the farms and in the shambas.

> The Kikuyu have lived in villages and small towns for a long time. The change to city life should be easy.

> We are farmers but many of us do not own any land and if we do, the plots are very small.

> We have learned some skills at school but we cannot use them in our local village.

> It is not far to Nairobi so we can get work there and still visit our village.

Activities

1 Read the following statements about Kenya's population. Write out the four statements which are correct.
   ● Kenya's population is spread evenly.
   ● Kenya's population is not spread evenly.
   ● The Maasai came from the Nile Valley and live in the south-west.
   ● The Maasai came from the south-west and live in the Nile Valley.
   ● The Kikuyu live in the north.
   ● The Kikuyu came from the south and west and live on higher land.
   ● Arabs and Indians live on the coast near Mombasa.

2 Make a copy of diagram **D** and complete it to show why the south of Kenya is more crowded than the north. For each box choose the correct word from the two given in brackets. 'Relief' has been done for you.

3 Imagine that you live in a small Kikuyu village and are about to migrate to Nairobi.
   a) Give at least three reasons for leaving your village.
   b) Give at least three advantages of living in Nairobi.
   Diagram **C** will help you to answer this question.

Summary

The distribution of population in Kenya is mainly affected by physical factors such as climate, water supply, relief and soil. Most people live in or near to the capital city of Nairobi.

D

Relief	Rainfall	Water supply			Temperature	Soils
Low			NORTH — Few people	KENYA		
High			SOUTH — Many people			
(High/Low)	(High/Low)	(Good/Poor)			(Hot/Warm)	(Good/Poor)

What does Nairobi look like to newcomers?

Like most cities in developing countries there are two sides to Nairobi. One side is seen by overseas visitors and the relatively few wealthy Kenyans. Photo **A** shows the most important building in Nairobi. It is the Kenyatta International Conference Centre, named after Jomo Kenyatta, the first president of Kenya. Around it, in central Nairobi, are tall, modern buildings and wide, tree-lined streets.

The other side of Nairobi is the one seen by most of the Kenyans who migrate from the surrounding rural areas. Many migrants move to live with family and friends already living in Nairobi. They share houses, food and even jobs. In time the newcomers may be able to construct their own homes in one of several **shanty** settlements found on the edge of the city (photo **B**).

A

B

C

Living in Kibera

Kibera is one shanty settlement. It is 6 kilometres and a 7 pence bus ride from the city centre. However, most inhabitants who wish to make that journey have to walk because they cannot afford the fare.

Houses in Kibera are built close together. Sometimes it is hard to squeeze between them. The walls are usually made from mud and the roofs from corrugated iron (photos **C** and **E**). Inside there is often only one room. Very few homes have water, electricity or sewage. Julius Mwenda is a 'rich man' by Kibera standards. He has a tap and can sell water to his neighbours. He also has a toilet but this is only emptied four times a year.

Sewage runs down the tracks between the houses (photo **C**). In the wet season rain mixes with the sewage making the tracks unusable, so small children are kept indoors for several weeks. In the dry season the tracks become very dusty. Photo **D** shows an open drain along a main sidetrack being cleared. What might happen to the sewage the next time it rains?

Kenya has one of the highest birth rates in the world. In Kibera it is not unusual for families to have more than ten children. Very few children can read or write as there is only one small school. Many suffer from a poor diet or malaria. Others catch diseases by drinking dirty water or playing in sewage (photo **C**).

People have to find their own way to earn money. Some have small stalls from which they sell food. Others, who have learnt a skill, may turn their houses into shops (photos **B** and **E**) or collect waste material and recycle it in small workshops.

D

E

Activities

1 Give three differences between photos **A** and **B**.

2 Map **F** shows the location of shanty settlements in Nairobi.
   a) How far is Kibera from the city centre?
   b) Which direction is Kibera from the city centre?
   c) Write out the following sentence using the correct word from the pair in brackets.

'Shanty settlements are areas of (good/poor) quality housing found at the (edge/middle) of the city on (good/poor) quality building land.'

3 Using photo **C**, list four problems of life in a shanty settlement.

4 List four ways that people living in a shanty settlement can earn money.

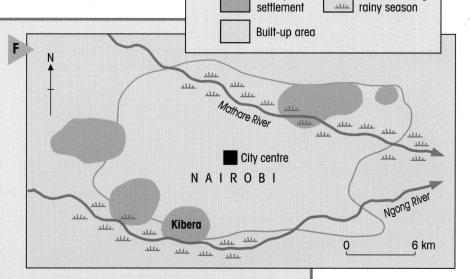

F

Key
Shanty settlement
Built-up area
Flooded during rainy season

N

Mathare River

■ City centre

N A I R O B I

Ngong River

Kibera

0   6 km

5 **a)** List four good points about living in Nairobi.
   b) Why is Nairobi described as having 'two sides'?

Summary

Cities in developing countries have two sides. Well-off people live and work in good conditions near to the city centre. Poor people often live and work in less pleasant shanty settlements a long way from the city centre.

What is a developing country?

By now you should be aware of many differences between living in Kenya and in your home region in the UK. These differences include ethnic groups, dress, housing, jobs, wealth and the quality of life. Kenya is an example of a **developing country**. What is a developing country? How is life in a developing country different from life in a developed country like the UK?

In the UK most, but not all, people earn a lot of money compared with those in a developing country. They live in good houses, have their own cars and videos and can afford good food and holidays. Compared with Kenya most people in Britain have a high **standard of living**. Kenya is considered to be 'poor' and the UK to be 'rich'. Most people see the difference in wealth as the main difference between a developing country and a developed country.

The wealth of a country is given by its **gross national product** (**GNP**). This is the total amount of money made by a country from its raw materials, its manufactured goods and its services.

Notice that GNP is always given in American dollars (US$). The total amount can then be divided by the total number of people living in that country. This gives the average amount of money available for every person living in the country.

By giving the GNP in US$ it is easy to compare different countries. Table **A** gives the average income (GNP) per person for five developing countries and three developed countries.

Apart from wealth there are many other ways of trying to measure the level of a country's development (table **B**).

A

	Country	GNP (US$ per person)
Developing countries	Bangladesh	220
	Brazil	3,020
	Egypt	660
	Kenya	270
	Peru	1,490
Developed countries	Japan	31,450
	UK	17,970
	USA	24,750

B

Jobs		Primary activities give most jobs in a developing country. A developed country has fewer primary activities and more secondary and service jobs.
Trade		A developing country usually has to sell raw materials at a low price and has to buy manufactured goods from developed countries at a high price.
Population		A developing country has a higher **birth** and **death rate** (page 70), more young children dying (high **infant mortality**), adults dying at a younger age (short **life expectancy**) and a faster population increase than a developed country.
Health		A developing country has less money to spend on training doctors and nurses and in providing hospitals and medicines.
Education		The large number of children and lack of money for schools in a developing country mean fewer people can read and write than in a developed country (low **literacy rate**).

The 'rich' North and the 'poor' South

What happens when the different methods used in table **B** to measure the level of development of a country are put together? The result is a group of mainly 'rich' countries which are found in the North and a group of mainly 'poor' countries which lie to the South. Map **C** shows this division.

C

North. Most countries north of the line are said to be *developed*.

The 'rich' North
- Large GNP
- Most jobs in industry and services
- Large amounts of trade
- Many doctors and hospitals
- Low birth and death rates
- Few children die young
- Slow population growth
- Long life
- Many schools

The 'poor' South
- Small GNP
- Most jobs in farming
- Small amounts of trade
- Few doctors and hospitals
- High birth and death rates
- Many children die young
- Rapid population growth
- Short life
- Few schools

South. Most countries south of the line are said to be *developing*.

Activities

1 Copy and complete star diagram **D** to show six possible ways of measuring the level of development of a country.

2 Draw a table and sort the information given in diagram **E** into two columns headed *Developing countries* and *Developed countries*.

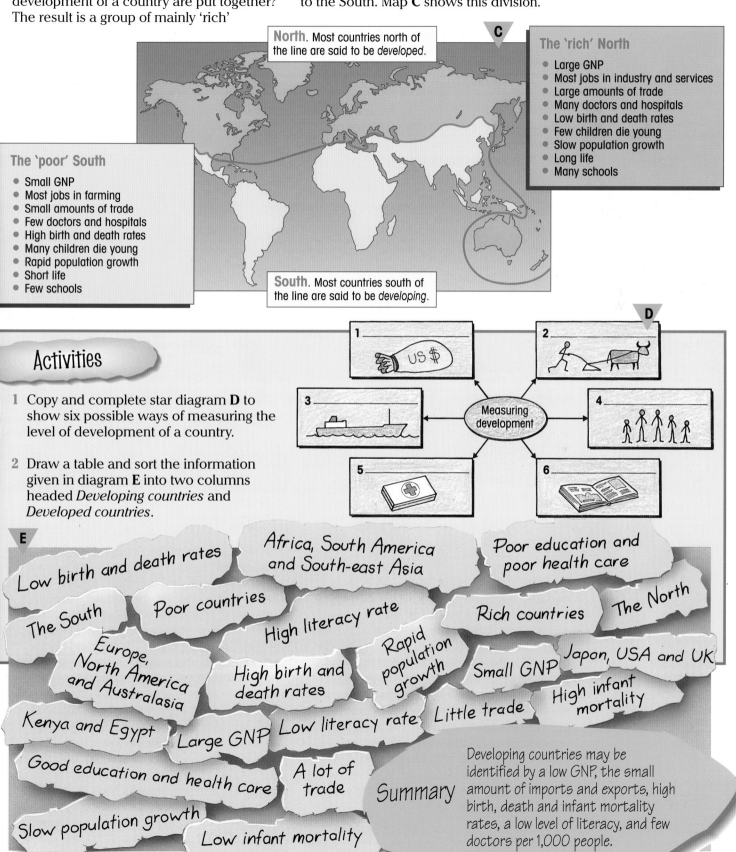

D

1 US $

2

3

Measuring development

4

5

6

E

Low birth and death rates

Africa, South America and South-east Asia

Poor education and poor health care

The South

Poor countries

High literacy rate

Rich countries

The North

Europe, North America and Australasia

High birth and death rates

Rapid population growth

Small GNP

Japan, USA and UK

High infant mortality

Kenya and Egypt

Large GNP

Low literacy rate

Little trade

Good education and health care

A lot of trade

Slow population growth

Low infant mortality

Summary

Developing countries may be identified by a low GNP, the small amount of imports and exports, high birth, death and infant mortality rates, a low level of literacy, and few doctors per 1,000 people.

Egypt – daily life in the Nile Delta

> Ahlan! A developing country is usually quite poor like Egypt in Africa.

'Ahlan' (hello) is the daily greeting given by Egyptians. Egypt is an **economically developing country** located in the north-east of Africa (see map **A** on page 90). By 'developing' we mean that it has less **capital** (money) and fewer services compared with a **developed** country like the UK. Egypt is said to be 'the gift of the Nile'. Without the River Nile the country would be desert.

Until the opening of the Aswan Dam in 1970 the river used to flood each year. This flooding spread water and fertile **silt** (soil) over the land. Near its mouth the silt blocked the main river channel, dividing it into two main rivers and many smaller ones. This is the large and very fertile **delta** of the River Nile.

A

B

How does the landscape and weather affect daily life in the Nile Delta?

The Nile Delta is completely flat. This is because every time the Nile flooded, it left two or three centimetres of silt. The black soil is now many metres deep. It is this flat land and fertile soil which make the delta one of the best farming areas in the world (photo **A**). It is the land, not money, which means wealth. The climate is warm in winter with only a few days' rain. Summers are very hot and completely dry. While temperatures are high enough for crops to grow all year there is not enough water without **irrigation**. Irrigation is when water is taken from the main river and led along small canals to the fields.

Houses

Most houses are either grouped together (**nucleated**) in large villages or spread out alongside roads and the many canals (**linear**). The walls of the square shaped houses are made from **adobe** brick (photo **B**). Adobe is mud taken from the river, cut into square blocks, and then baked under the hot rays of the sun. An outside staircase, supported by beams from palm trees, leads to the roof. The roof is often a thatch made from date palm leaves. It is flat as sloped roofs are only needed in places where it rains. Doors and windows are small. They have wooden shutters which can be closed when sand and dust is blown from the Sahara Desert. The houses have neither fresh water nor a sewage system. However, some now get electricity from the power station at the Aswan Dam.

Dress

The **fellahin** (farmers) wear a long robe called a *gallabiya* (photo **C**). It is made from cotton that is grown locally. It is loose-fitting for coolness in the hot climate. The *kefiyeh* is an Arab head-dress worn as protection against the sun.

Daily life

Apart from a few hours at midday when the sun is too hot, the fellahin spend all day in their fields. It is back-breaking work. Wooden ploughs pulled by buffalo, and spades and hoes, are the only tools. Seed is scattered by hand and the harvest is collected by hand. Each day silt has to be removed from the irrigation channels and water diverted to the many small fields. Women are equally busy. Clothes are washed in the river and drinking water fetched from the river and canals. Food has to be cooked and surplus crops taken to the town for sale (photos **C** and **D**). Women carry water in pots and food in baskets balanced on their heads. The river is also used for bathing, sewage and fishing.

Diet

This is mainly rice, bread, beans, fruit and vegetables, all grown on farms in the delta. Chicken and pigeon are the main meat.

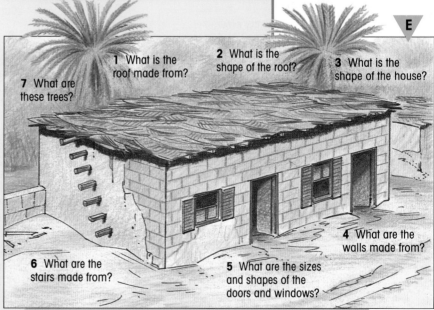

Activities

1 Give two facts about a developing country.
  b) In which continent is Egypt?
  c) Which river flows through Egypt?

2 Unscramble the following words to give eight uses of the River Nile and the canals leading from it.

irritagion	pranstort	wesage	ashwing
oils	singhif	thingab	dinkring rawet

3 Sketch **E** is a house in the Nile Delta. Draw the house and add labels by answering the questions on the diagram.

4 **a)** Imagine you belong to a family living in the Nile Delta. List the jobs and activities that you and your family may do in a typical day.
  b) Underline those things done by women.
  c) Why is nothing done at midday?

E

1 What is the roof made from?
2 What is the shape of the roof?
3 What is the shape of the house?
7 What are these trees?
4 What are the walls made from?
6 What are the stairs made from?
5 What are the sizes and shapes of the doors and windows?

Summary Landscape, weather and wealth all affect the family life, housing, clothing, land use and diet of people living in the Nile Delta.

Why is Egypt's population unevenly spread?

The present-day inhabitants of Egypt are descended from two main groups of people who arrived in the country from opposite directions (map **A**).

● Most Egyptians are Arabs who settled in the Lower Nile Valley and its Delta. They came from the north-east.
● A smaller number of Nubians live along the banks of the Nile in Upper Egypt. They came from the south.

How do physical conditions affect Egypt's population distribution?

Physical factors account for the Nile Valley and Delta being densely populated (areas ① and ② on map **B**), and the rest of Egypt being very sparsely populated (area ③ on map **B**). We have already seen that without the River Nile Egypt would be a desert. Life is very difficult without water. The result is that 96 out of every 100 Egyptians live within a few kilometres of the Nile and its

water. Map **B** links the differences in population density with differences in rainfall, water supply, relief, soil and vegetation.

Ancient Egypt was one of the world's oldest civilisations. Its rulers, the Pharaohs, built the pyramids.

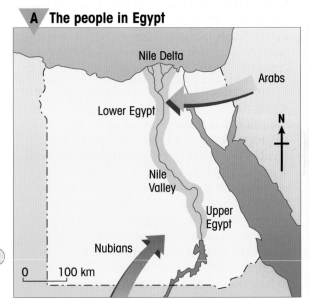

A   The people in Egypt

Nile Delta
Arabs
Lower Egypt
Nubians
Nile Valley
Upper Egypt
N
0   100 km

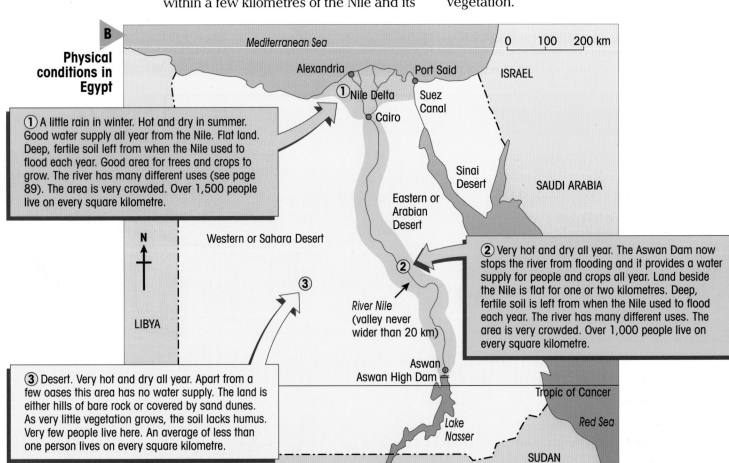

B

Physical conditions in Egypt

Mediterranean Sea

0   100   200 km

Alexandria   Port Said   ISRAEL
① Nile Delta   Suez Canal
Cairo

① A little rain in winter. Hot and dry in summer. Good water supply all year from the Nile. Flat land. Deep, fertile soil left from when the Nile used to flood each year. Good area for trees and crops to grow. The river has many different uses (see page 89). The area is very crowded. Over 1,500 people live on every square kilometre.

Sinai Desert   SAUDI ARABIA

Eastern or Arabian Desert

N

Western or Sahara Desert

③

② Very hot and dry all year. The Aswan Dam now stops the river from flooding and it provides a water supply for people and crops all year. Land beside the Nile is flat for one or two kilometres. Deep, fertile soil is left from when the Nile used to flood each year. The river has many different uses. The area is very crowded. Over 1,000 people live on every square kilometre.

River Nile (valley never wider than 20 km)

②

LIBYA

③ Desert. Very hot and dry all year. Apart from a few oases this area has no water supply. The land is either hills of bare rock or covered by sand dunes. As very little vegetation grows, the soil lacks humus. Very few people live here. An average of less than one person lives on every square kilometre.

Aswan
Aswan High Dam

Tropic of Cancer

Red Sea

Lake Nasser

SUDAN

Present-day movements of population

In all developing countries there is a large movement of people from the countryside to the towns (rural-to-urban migration, see page 73). In Egypt it is mainly people who live in the Nile Delta who move. To a visitor the Delta appears to be good place to live (photo **A**, page 88). It is one of the few parts of Egypt with roads. It has the best farmland and water supply in the country and the environment seems clean and pleasant compared with urban areas. To those living there, especially those still at school or just starting a family, it is less attractive. Sketch **C** gives some of the reasons why many people living in the Nile Delta want to move to Cairo, the capital city of Egypt.

C

Egypt has one of the highest birth rates in the world. The average family size is over 6 people. There are too many of us to find jobs on farms.

We are farmers but many of us do not own land and if we do the plots are very small.

We have lived in villages and small towns for a long time. The change to city life should be easy.

It is not far to Cairo so we can get work there and still visit our village.

Cairo has big, modern buildings which include hospitals, shops, cinemas and a university.

We have learned some skills at school but we cannot use them in our home village.

Activities

1 Read the following six statements about Egypt's population. Write out the four statements which are correct.
   - Egypt's population is evenly spread.
   - Egypt's population is not evenly spread.
   - Most people live close to the River Nile.
   - Most Egyptians are Arabs who came from the north-east.
   - Most Egyptians are Nubians who came from the south.
   - Nubians are a small group of people who live in the south of Egypt.

2 Make a copy of diagram **D** and complete it to show why places near to the River Nile are much more crowded than places away from the River Nile.

3 Imagine that you live in a village in the Nile Delta and are about to migrate to Cairo.
   a) Give at least three reasons for leaving your village.
   b) Give at least three advantages of living in Cairo.
   Sketch **C** will help you to answer this question.

Summary

The distribution of population in Egypt is mainly affected by physical factors such as climate, water supply, relief and soil. Most people live in the Nile Valley and its Delta, or in the capital city of Cairo.

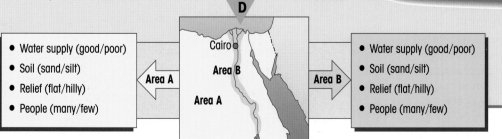

D

- Water supply (good/poor)
- Soil (sand/silt)
- Relief (flat/hilly)
- People (many/few)

Area A

Cairo
Area B
Area A

Area B

- Water supply (good/poor)
- Soil (sand/silt)
- Relief (flat/hilly)
- People (many/few)

What does Cairo look like to a newcomer?

Like most cities in developing countries there are two sides to Cairo. One side is seen by overseas visitors and the relatively few wealthy Egyptians. Photo **A** shows one of the most important buildings in Cairo. It is the Cairo Tower built on an island in the Nile and shaped like one of the lotus flowers which grow in that river. Around it, in central Cairo and extending west to the Pyramids, are tall modern buildings which include many luxury hotels.

The other side of Cairo is the one seen by most Egyptians who migrate from the rural areas. Many migrants move to live with family and friends already living in 'Old Cairo' (photo **B**). They crowd into two-roomed homes within tall blocks of flats or camp in any empty space on the already overcrowded roof-tops. It is claimed that nearly 5,000 new migrants arrive in Cairo each week. This means that each year almost as many people move into the capital as live in either Southampton or Newcastle.

Living in the 'City of the Dead'

The 'City of the Dead' is a huge Muslim cemetery full of tombs and mosques. Many homeless migrants have found that these tombs provide a clean place to live. Stone for the tombs came from the same nearby quarries that were used for building the Pyramids. Most tombs have one room. Being a cemetery, there was no need for a water supply, a sewage system or electricity. The 'city' has become a **shanty** settlement with over one million people living there (photo **C**).

The Cairo authorities, faced with so many newcomers, find it impossible to provide extra homes for them. They have now decided that it is easier and cheaper to provide water and electricity for this area than to build tall blocks of flats. Yet within the 'City of the Dead' there is a thriving community. It includes a large, cheap market (photo **D**) and many small workshops. Often the workshops are just the front of a house opened up (photo **E**). Dust, animals and washing are everywhere.

Egypt has a high birth rate. Most families living in the 'City of the Dead' have more than six children. There are not enough resources to teach everyone to read and write nor to provide them with good health care.

Cairo's problems

Apart from a lack of housing Cairo has many other problems. Most of these result from rapid migration. Traffic is very noisy, causes pollution and jams the narrow streets. The many small workshops also pollute the air. These are set up in houses, on roof-tops and in backyards. Despite these workshops one in three people do not have a full-time job. Donkey carts can only collect a little of the city's rubbish. Disease can spread quickly. The Cairo authorities are building many new houses, roads, schools and hospitals but they are unable to keep up with the thousands of newcomers arriving in the city.

Activities

1 Give three differences between photos **A** and **B**.

2 Copy out and complete star diagram **F** to describe a typical 'house' in the 'City of the Dead'.

3 Match the following beginnings with their correct endings to describe some of Cairo's problems.

F
No w _____
House in the City of the Dead
Roof made from _____
No e _____
Walls made from _____
No s _____
Number of rooms _____

Cars, buses, lorries and donkey carts	a little of the city's rubbish.
Many houses do not have	cause noise and pollute the air.
Despite the many workshops	for the 5,000 newcomers each week.
The traffic and workshops	block the narrow streets.
There are not enough houses	only one in three people have full-time jobs.
Donkey carts can only collect	water, electricity or sewage disposal.

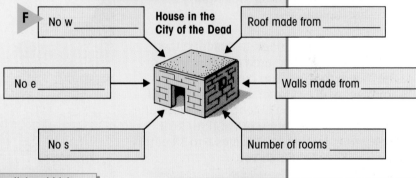

4 **a)** Using photos **A** and **G**, list four good points about living in Cairo.
   b) Why is Cairo described as having 'two sides'?

Summary Cities in developing countries have two sides. The well-off, who have a choice, usually live in pleasant conditions. The poor are left with the worst places.

The river enquiry

The Pennine Way is one of Britain's best known long distance walks. It stretches some 410 km (256 miles) from the Derbyshire Peak District northwards to the Cheviots and into Scotland. One of the walk's most interesting sections is in Upper Teesdale. Here the trail follows the River Tees through some wild and impressive scenery. At one point it overlooks High Force, one of Britain's finest waterfalls.

Every year the Upper Teesdale area receives more and more visitors. Some people have suggested that a small pamphlet explaining the features of the area would be helpful. This would enable walkers and tourists to understand their surroundings and help them enjoy their stay in the area. Your task is to produce the pamphlet by answering the enquiry question below.

To do this you will need to describe the main features of the area and find out how they were formed. You could work by yourself, with a partner or even in a small group. You might be able to use a computer to word process your work and make it look more professional. Pages 6 to 13 of this book will be helpful to you.

How does the River Tees shape the land?

Your aims for this piece of work are:
● to answer the enquiry question
● to produce an information pamphlet for use by walkers and other visitors to Upper Teesdale
● to describe and explain the main physical features of the area
● to make your pamphlet attractive, interesting, helpful and simple to understand.

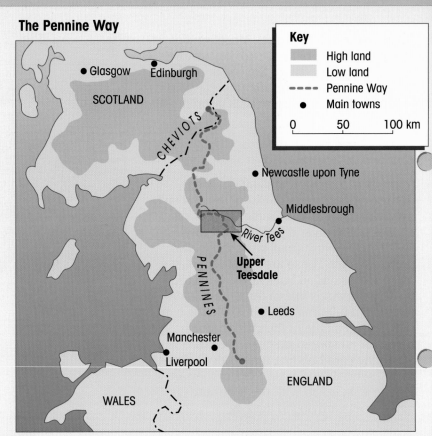

The Pennine Way

94

1 Introduction – what is the area like, and how can rivers shape the land?

You will need to use maps and writing here. Diagrams and even cartoons might also help.

a) First say what the Pennine Way is and show where it is located.

b) Next describe Upper Teesdale. You will need to:
- say whereabouts it is
- describe the scenery
- suggest why it is a popular area for visitors.

The text and map on page 94 and the sketch below will help you with this. Try to use the words on the notice board in your description.

c) Finally, describe how rivers can shape the land through erosion, transportation and deposition processes.

UPPER TEESDALE

highland area. wild. valley. moorland. rural. beautiful. waterfall. Pennine Way. High Force. scattered farms. gorge.

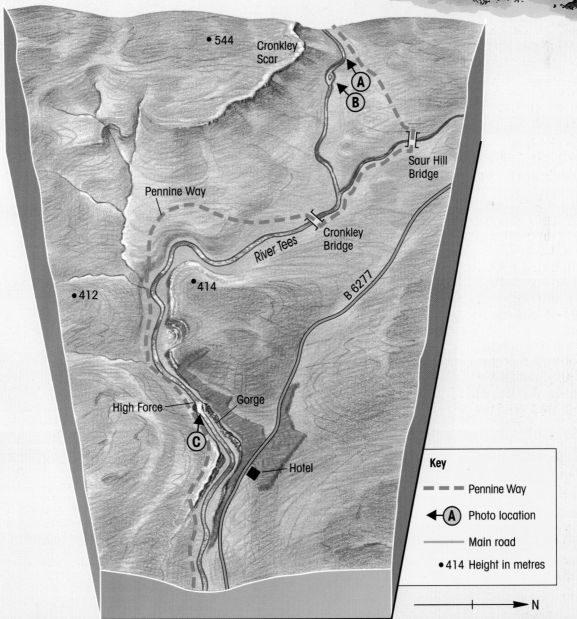

• 544
Cronkley Scar
Ⓐ
Ⓑ
Saur Hill Bridge
Pennine Way
River Tees
Cronkley Bridge
• 414
B 6277
• 412
High Force
Gorge
Ⓒ
Hotel

Key

- - - Pennine Way
◀Ⓐ Photo location
— Main road
•414 Height in metres

N

A

The river on this bend is about 25 metres wide with a depth of no more than half a metre. The deepest water is on the right of the photo.

2 What are the main landform features and how were they formed?

a) Look carefully at photos **A**, **B** and **C**, which show a river bend, an area that floods, and High Force waterfall and gorge.

b) For each one in turn describe the feature and explain the river processes that helped form it. You could use labelled sketches, cross-section drawings, block diagrams and writing here.

Try to present your work in a clear and interesting way. It is important that your readers find your work attractive and are able to understand fully what you are showing them.

B

At times of flood, the river here is almost 300 metres wide. The valley floor is made up of alluvium (silt) and boulders of all sizes.

C

At High Force the River Tees plunges down a vertical cliff of over 20 metres. The wearing away of the rock by the falls has left a steep-sided gorge. This is some 700 metres in length.

D

Hard whinstone

Soft limestone

Plunge pool

3 Conclusion

This should be a summary to go at the end of your information pamphlet. There could be two parts to it. Together they should answer the question set by the enquiry question.

a) First you need to describe briefly the three main landform features of the area, and show their location. You could do this by adding labels to a map or sketch like the one on page 95. You should write no more than about 20 words for each label.

b) Secondly you should write a paragraph to explain how the River Tees has helped shape the land in this area.

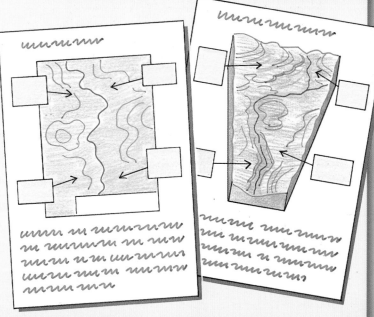

This enquiry is concerned with locating a factory. You will find pages 36 to 45 of this book helpful as you work through the enquiry.

In December 1994 the first Toyota car to be made in Europe was driven out of the new factory at Burnaston near Derby. This event followed years of planning and preparation by the Toyota company.

One of the most important decisions that had to be made in the planning process was where to locate the factory. Toyota gave the responsibility of choosing the best site to a small team of experts.

The team began by making a list of location factors for the new factory. They then drew up a shortlist of sites that met the basic requirements. Next they investigated the advantages and disadvantages of each site before finally choosing what they considered to be the best site.

Some of the location factors that the team considered are shown in the drawing below. On the next page are ten possible sites along with information about each one.

Your task in this enquiry is to suggest:
● why Toyota chose the Burnaston site
● how they came to make that choice
● whether their choice was the best one.

> **Did Toyota choose the best site for their new factory?**

Possible sites for the Toyota factory

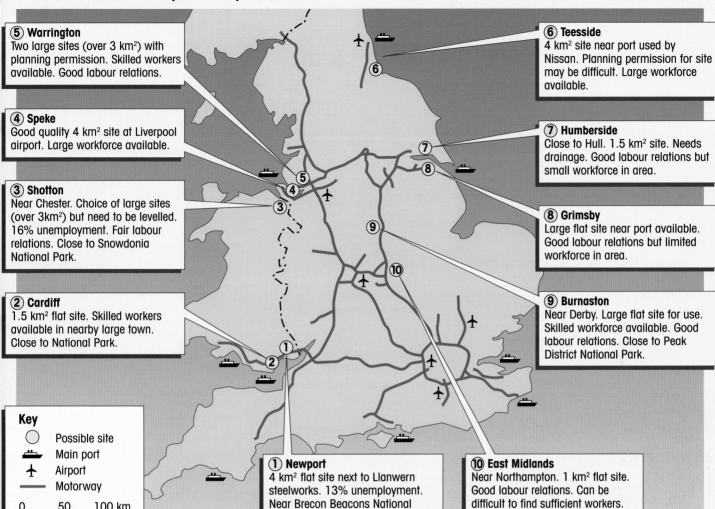

⑤ Warrington
Two large sites (over 3 km²) with planning permission. Skilled workers available. Good labour relations.

④ Speke
Good quality 4 km² site at Liverpool airport. Large workforce available.

③ Shotton
Near Chester. Choice of large sites (over 3km²) but need to be levelled. 16% unemployment. Fair labour relations. Close to Snowdonia National Park.

② Cardiff
1.5 km² flat site. Skilled workers available in nearby large town. Close to National Park.

⑥ Teesside
4 km² site near port used by Nissan. Planning permission for site may be difficult. Large workforce available.

⑦ Humberside
Close to Hull. 1.5 km² site. Needs drainage. Good labour relations but small workforce in area.

⑧ Grimsby
Large flat site near port available. Good labour relations but limited workforce in area.

⑨ Burnaston
Near Derby. Large flat site for use. Skilled workforce available. Good labour relations. Close to Peak District National Park.

① Newport
4 km² flat site next to Llanwern steelworks. 13% unemployment. Near Brecon Beacons National Park.

⑩ East Midlands
Near Northampton. 1 km² flat site. Good labour relations. Can be difficult to find sufficient workers. Near pleasant countryside.

Key
- ⬭ Possible site
- ⛴ Main port
- ✈ Airport
- — Motorway

0   50   100 km

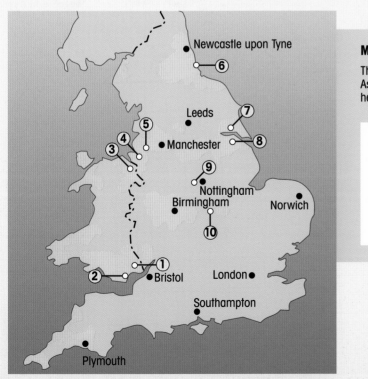

Main towns and Assisted Areas

The government gives help to industry in Assisted Areas. This may include loans, grants, help with training and provision of services.

Key
- ⬭─o Possible site
- ● Main town
- ▒ Assisted Area

0   100 km

1 Introduction – what is the enquiry about?

You could use diagrams, maps, writing or lists here.

a) Describe what you have to find out in the enquiry.
b) Give a brief background to the new Toyota factory and describe where it is.
c) Explain how the best site may be chosen.

DID TOYOTA CHOOSE THE BEST SITE FOR THEIR NEW FACTORY

2 What are the location factors?

Draw a star diagram like the one here. Add about ten words of description to each factor. The diagram on page 98 will help you.

Site

Communications

Workforce (labour)

Government aid

Location factors for the Toyota car factory

Environment

Matrix for choosing the best site for the Toyota car factory

Give a score of **0** to **4** for each site

4 if the site is **excellent**
3 if the site is **very good**
2 if the site is **good** but has faults
1 if the site is **poor** and only just acceptable
0 if the site is **unsatisfactory**

Score **2** if there is **no information** given

	Newport ①	Cardiff ②	Shotton ③	Speke ④	Warrington ⑤	Teesside ⑥	Humberside ⑦	Grimsby ⑧	Burnaston ⑨	East Midlands ⑩
Size of site										
Quality of site										
Near to motorway										
Near to port										
Near to airport										
Skilled workers nearby										
Good labour relations										
Government help available										
Near to attractive countryside										
Total										

Which is the best site?

a) Make a larger copy of the matrix opposite.

b) Look carefully at the information on page 99. For the first location factor give a score for each site. Do the same for each of the other location factors. (The location factors are described more fully on the diagram on page 98.)

c) Add up the scores in each column. The one with the highest total will be the best site.

d) List the ten sites in order of their total scores. Put the best at the top of the list.

Conclusion

a) Which are the three best sites? List the main advantages of each one.

b) Suggest why Toyota chose the Burnaston site rather than the other two.

c) If the Burnaston site had not been available, would the other sites have been satisfactory? Give reasons for your answer.

d) **Either**
- Draw a simple sketch of the photo below. Add information to the boxes to explain why Burnaston is a good site for the Toyota car factory. Page 99 and your completed matrix will help you with this.

Or
- Write a report for Head Office in Japan about the Burnaston site. In the report describe the main features of the site and explain why it is a good location for the Toyota car factory.

The Toyota factory at Burnaston near Derby

Workforce (labour)

Site

Government aid

Communications

Environment

Glossary

A

Acid rain	Rain water containing chemicals which come from burning fossil fuels. *60*
Agriculture	The growing of crops and rearing of animals. *24*
Alluvium	Sometimes called silt. Fine soil left behind after a river floods. *13*
Arable farming	The growing of crops. *24, 32, 33*
Arch	An opening through a rock. *14*
Assembling	Putting together manufactured parts to make things such as computers or cars. *34, 39*
Attractive countryside	Areas of pleasant scenery such as mountains rivers, lakes and coasts. *50*

B

Bay	A wide curved inlet of a sea or lake. *14*
Beach	An area of sand or pebbles along a coast. *15*
Biological weathering	The breakdown of rock by plants and animals. *5*
Birth rate	The number of people being born for each 1,000 of the population. *70, 85, 86, 93*
Business parks	New offices built in pleasant surroundings on the edge of cities. *42*

C

Capital	The amount of money belonging to a country, factory or a person. *27, 28, 78, 88*
Chemical weathering	The breakdown of rock by chemical action. *5*
Clean-up	A method of getting rid of pollution. *17, 19*
Commercial farming	When farm produce is sold for a profit. *27, 80*
Conservation	The protection of the environment. *48*
Conservationists	People who care for and look after the environment. *50, 53, 61*
Construction industry	Building and repairing places, e.g. houses, factories and roads. *34*
Cross-section	A view at right-angles across a landform. *12*
Current	The flow of water in a certain direction. *6*

D

Death rate	The number of people dying per 1,000 of the population. *70, 86*
Delta	A flat area of alluvium or silt at the mouth of a river. *88*
Densely populated	An area that is crowded. *64, 67, 82, 90*
Density	A measure of how close together people live in an area. *64*
Deposition	The laying down of material carried by rivers, sea, ice or wind. *7*
Deposition landforms	Landscape features made up of material that has been laid down. *15*
Developed country	A country which has a lot of money, many services and a high standard of living. *78, 87, 88*
Developing country	A country which is often quite poor, has few services and a low standard of living. *78, 86, 87, 88*

E

Economic activity	A primary, secondary or tertiary industry. *20*
Endangered species	Wildlife in danger of becoming extinct. *52*
Energy	The power to do something and to give off heat. *35, 56*
Environment	The natural or physical surroundings where people, plants and animals live. *48, 50, 55, 60, Unit 4*
Erosion	The wearing away and removal of rock, soil, etc. by rivers, sea, ice and wind. *4, 6, 7*
Erosion landforms	Landscape features resulting from the wearing away of rock. *14*
Exploitation	The selfish use or development of something for our own benefit, without considering how it will affect other people and the environment. *58*
Extensive farming	Farms which cover a large area of land but employ few people. *28, 29*
Extinct	Wildlife which can no longer be found living on earth. *52*

F

Factories	Places where things are made from natural resources and raw materials. *34 and Unit 3*
Farm woodland scheme	Money given to farmers to plant trees instead of crops. *33*
Flood plain	The flat area at the bottom of a valley which is often flooded. *13*
Food mountains and lakes	Surplus supplies of farm products. *33*
Fossil fuels	Fuels from the remains of plants or ancient life. *56, 60*

	Frost shattering	A form of weathering where water in cracks freezes and expands to split or shatter the rock. *4*
G	**Global warming**	The warming of the earth's atmosphere by burning fossil fuels and releasing carbon dioxide. *60*
	Gorge	A steep-sided valley. *10*
	Greenfield sites	Land found on the edge of an urban area which has not yet been built on. *42*
	Gross national product (GNP)	The wealth of a country. Its total income divided by its total population. *86*
H	**Headland**	A part of the coastline that juts out into the sea and usually ends in a cliff. *14*
	Hedgerows	Bushes and small trees that are used as field boundaries. *30, 50*
	High-tech industries	Industries using advanced machines and skilled people, e.g. computers and electronics. *42*
	Historic sites	Important old settlements and buildings which are interesting to people. *50*
I	**Industrialised**	Using machines and power (energy) to make things. *38*
	Infant mortality rate	The number of children out of every 1,000 born alive that die before they reach the age of one year. *86*
	Information technology (IT)	The exchange of ideas and information. *42, 43*
	Intensive farming	Farms which cover small areas but which use either many people or a lot of capital. No land is wasted. *28*
	International migration	The movement of people from one country to another. *73*
	Irrigated	Land that has been artificially watered. *27, 88*
L	**Labour**	Workers. Employed people. *28, 36*
	Landscape	The scenery. What the land looks like. *4, 30*
	Life expectancy	The average number of years a person can expect to live. *86*
	Literacy rate	The number of people who can read and write. *86*
	Load	The material carried by a river. *9*
M	**Market**	A place where raw materials and goods are sold. A group of people who buy raw materials or goods. *25, 36, 39*
	Market gardening	The growing of fruit, vegetables and flowers. *27, 28*
	Meander	A large bend in a river. *13*
	Migrant workers	People who live in one country and travel each day to work in another. *74*
	Migration	The movement of people from one place to another to live or to work. *72, 73, 74, 76, 82, 84, 91*
	Mining	The extraction of minerals from deep under the ground, e.g. coal, iron ore. *21*
	Mixed farming	The growing of crops and rearing of animals on the same farm. *24, 32*
	Monsoon	A seasonal wind in India and South-east Asia. During the wet monsoon the wind brings lots of rain from the sea. During the dry monsoon the wind blows from the land and the weather is dry. *26*
N	**Natural increase**	The difference between birth and death rates. *71*
	Natural resources	Raw materials which are obtained from the environment, e.g. water, coal, soil. *20*
	Negative factors	Things that discourage people from living in a place. *66, 67*
	Non-renewable resources	Resources that can only be used once, e.g. coal, oil. *56, 60*
O	**Onion-skin weathering**	The breakdown of rock by heating and cooling which causes the surface layers to peel off. *4*
P	**Pastoral farming**	The rearing of animals. *24*
	Pastoralists	Farmers who look after herds of animals. *78*
	Plantation	Large farmed area often of one crop which is sold for cash. *80*
	Plunge pool	A hollow at the base of a waterfall caused by erosion. *10, 97*
	Polar regions	Cold areas of the world near to the North and South Poles. *68*
	Pollution	Noise, dirt and other harmful substances produced by people and machines which spoil an area. *16, 46, 47, 48, 49, 61*
	Population distribution	How people are spread out over an area. *64, 66, 82, 90*
	Population explosion	A sudden rapid rise in the number of people. *70*
	Population growth	The increase in the number of people in an area. *70*
	Population growth rate	A measure of how quickly the number of people in an area increases. *70*

	Positive factors	Things that encourage people to live in an area. *66, 67*
	Power	Energy needed to work machines and to produce electricity. *36*
	Primary activity	Collecting and using natural resources, e.g. farming, fishing, forestry and mining. *20, 86*
	Pull factors	Things that attract people to live in an area. *73*
	Push factors	Things that make people want to leave an area. *73*
Q	**Quarry**	Where rock is cut from the surface of the land. *21, 22, 61*
R	**Raw materials**	Natural resources which are used to make things. *20, 36, 38, 49*
	Recycling	Turning waste into something which is usable again. *56*
	Redevelop	To knock everything down and start all over again. *40, 56, 57*
	Renewable resources	Resources which can be used over and over again. *56, 57*
	Resources	Things which can be useful to people. They may be natural like coal and iron ore, or of other value like money and skilled workers. *46, 49*
	River cliff	The steep slope cut into a valley side by erosion on the outside of a river bend. *12*
	Rural-to-urban migration	The movement of people from the countryside to the towns and cities. *73, 83, 91*
S	**Science park**	An estate of high-tech industries having links with a university. *42*
	Seasonal jobs	Employment that lasts for only part of the year. *74*
	Secondary activities	Where natural resources are turned into goods which we can use. *34, 86*
	Set-aside land	Scheme where farmers are paid for not farming their land. *33*
	Sewage	Waste material from homes and industry. *16, 17, 84*
	Shanty settlement	A collection of shacks and poor quality housing which often lack electricity, a water supply and sewage disposal. *84, 92*
	Silt	Sometimes called alluvium. Fine soil left behind after a river floods. *13, 26, 88, 89*
	Site	The place where a settlement or a factory is located. *36, 44*
	Soil erosion	The removal of soil by wind or water. *31*
	Sparsely populated	An area that has few people living in it. *64, 67, 82, 90*
	Spit	A long narrow tongue of sand and shingle which grows out from the shoreline. *15*
	Spoil tip	Piles of waste material left after mining and quarrying. *21, 22*
	Stack	A pillar of rock on a sea coast separated from the mainland by erosion. *14*
	Standard of living	How well-off a person or a country is. *74, 86*
	Subsidies	Money given to farmers and industries by a government. *33*
	Subsistence	Growing just enough food for your own needs with nothing left over to sell. *26, 80*
T	**Technology**	New ways of using resources and developing new equipment. *25, 62*
	Temporary migrants	People who live and work in a country for a short time before returning home. *74*
	Thermal power	Electricity produced by burning fossil fuels. *60*
	Trade	The movement of goods and services between countries. *86*
	Transport	Ways of moving people and goods from one place to another. *36, 45, 62*
	Transportation	The movement of eroded material by rivers, sea, ice and wind. *7*
V	**V-shaped valley**	A valley which has been eroded by a river so that its shape from one side to the other looks like a letter V. *8, 9*
W	**Waterfall**	A sudden fall of water over a steep drop. *10*
	Weathering	The action of the weather, plants and animals on rocks. The rocks are broken down without being removed. *4, 6, 8*
	Wetlands	Marshy areas which are a habitat for wildlife. *30, 50*
	Wilderness	A place which has not been developed by people and is still in its natural state. *54*
	Wildlife habitats	The homes of plant and animals. *50, 58*